CW00551396

The Temperaments and the Arts

Their Relation and Function in Waldorf Pedagogy

by

Magda Lissau

A W S N A

Published by:
The Association of Waldorf Schools of North America
3911 Bannister Road
Fair Oaks, CA 95628

Title: The Temperaments and the Arts
Their Relation and Function in Waldorf Pedagogy
Author: Magda Lissau
© 2003 by AWSNA
ISBN # 1-888365-43-9
Editor: David Mitchell
Proofreader: Ann Erwin
Cover: Hallie Wootan and Susan Spaulding
Originally a private printing, Chicago: 1983; fully revised and re-edited 2003
Originally distributed by: St. George Book Service. Inc., Spring Valley, NY

Curriculum Series
The Publications Committee of AWSNA is pleased to bring forward this publication as part of its Curriculum Series. The thoughts and ideas represented herein are solely those of the author and do not necessarily represent any implied criteria set by AWSNA. It is our intention to stimulate as much writing and thinking as possible about our curriculum, including diverse views. Please contact us with feedback on this publication as well as requests for future work.

David S. Mitchell
For the Publications Committee
AWSNA

Acknowledgements

At the occasion of the first edition of this book, much gratitude was expressed to the three master teachers whom I was fortunate enough to meet early in my teaching career: Alex Baum, Hans van der Stok, and Max Stibbe.

I also extend my thanks to Werner Glas and Rosemary Gebert of the Waldorf Institute of Mercy College, Southfield, MI, for much needed advice and encouragement while these pages were written; to Phyllis Morris and Olga Wierbicki for their invaluable help in editing. Last but not least to my former and present students who taught me most of all.

At the occasion of the new edition, much gratitude needs to be expressed to all those whose comments have encouraged me to undertake the task of preparing a second edition. Much thanks is due to AWSNA Publications and David Mitchell for his professionalism in making this edition into a far more visually pleasing and readable book than it was before. The many colleagues, teacher development students, and others active in the Waldorf movement are too numerous to mention by name. May these modest pages be of help in their professional striving.

— Magda Lissau

Table Of Contents

Part Three:
    BRIDGES OF UNDERSTANDING

PART ONE

THE LANGUAGE OF THE TEMPERAMENTS
IN COSMOS AND HUMANITY

Chapter One

The Four Elements in Cosmos and Humanity

But there is nothing in this world that is not permeated by the etheric world. [1]

— Rudolf Steiner

The etheric world is the mediator between the higher spiritual worlds and all that is manifest in physical form. The etheric forces work in both nature and human beings. In the human being they are the nexus of life forces sustaining our life. Let us attempt to trace their activity in the different states of matter, which in earlier ages were known as the four elements.

Individual and world—microcosm and macrocosm—are intimately related to each other. One is the reflection, the inversion, the reciprocal image of the other. Any understanding of humanity eludes us until we learn anew to look into the world of nature. Looking at the phenomena of nature, our perception and understanding may grow to become a sensing of the spiritual forces and beings at work behind these very phenomena. Only then are we in a position to begin to develop an understanding for the human being. So let us find first the archetypal picture underlying both the human temperaments in individuals and the elements in nature.

Earth

Stillness, coolness, passivity—thus does the solidity of matter confine its form and limit each object with crystalline clarity. Measure and weight, density and gravity, impermeability, and inertia determine the solid bodies of the earth.

In the stillness of the crystal world of geometric space the princess waits, pale, beautiful, yet asleep, still untouched and unmoved by future destiny. She awaits disenchantment, hidden by a dry and brittle crust, which preserves the solitude of the self within. Great clarity of thought may abide in these depths. Possibly an astute observer of mathematical bent inhabits the quiet caves formed of earthy, stony, rocky, impenetrably firm and hard substance.

Be they minute or massive, the earthy shapes are concentrated, contracted. Dark and dull from afar, they often glimmer in surprising colors at a closer look. Within, the light may find a way, may be reflected, and may shine through as concentrated beam. Great effort is needed to impress and shape this solid earthy element. Yet, once an impact is made, once change has been effected, it lasts.

The earthy element is the solid basis of our physical existence. The crust of the earth carries its life, carries plants, human beings and animals. The ground supporting our every step—this encompassing stony mantle of the earth—consists, amazingly enough, of innumerable separate shapes and bodies, from tectonic plate to pegmatite and grain of sand. All are separate entities. An overwhelming diversification of shape and form abounds in the earthy realm.

Fire

Fire is the all-pervading gift of the gods, wrested from the heavens as was told in olden myths. It is scourge, inspiration and healer, from the homely fire of the hearth to the strong blaze of the smith, the devastating conflagration of a forest fire and the gentle flame of the candle—all are fire in endless variation.

The fiery bird of legend showers multi-colored sparks of flame upon us—a fascinating play of motility and color, each moment unique and totally unpredictable. It is this spectacle of flames which gladdens and warms our hearts with deepest joy.

Our whole being expands when we watch fire. Fire, too, expands all forms, as it consumes them in a blaze. It expands them beyond the borders of the material world, destroying the earthy element's hold on their form. Thus fire becomes the essence of mutability, the furnace for the transformation of the old into the new. We are enveloped and comforted by its strength. It is our ally in subduing nature and forging her substance anew according to our will and ingenuity.

Earth and fire are diametrically opposed: heat and cold, expansion into space, contraction into the center, flight from the earth, chained by weight. Our heart leaps with joy as we see the flame leap upwards, reach and burst forth into the heights, back into the world of the gods on high. Our heart contracts when weighted down in the grip of icy cold. It is pressed down when we are sunk to our very depths in pondering thought.

Water

The all-suffusing, ever-moving sphere of water encloses the globe with rolling waves from horizon to horizon. It levels as it calms, or bares long-forgotten secrets in angry waves. Surface tension is great—it closes off the inner deeps from the prying eye, the curious probe. Forever it strives to find its lowest level and presses down upon the mineral earth with increasing force. The surface is impressionable—at least it seems this way as the slightest breeze causes ripples to flit over its surface.

The running brook, gently following the slope to river, stream, and sea, delights us with its chattering and murmuring, as it gives life to all nature along its banks. The waters, which flow and merge, ripple, and reflect as well as nourish, are the basis of all the life of nature. The being of water is a veritable Proteus of rainbow-hued disguise.

Water's close relation with air is apparent in the thick mists of morning, in the rising clouds and the falling rains—in the constant change between rising and falling. Water leaps the surface tension into the air and joins the streaming, blowing, flowing currents of air in its minutest droplets. Or it condenses into heavy drops, rushing to earth, to join the hugest drop of all—the watery sphere. The spherical shape is its signature form. The surface tension of each drop, both great and small, guards and preserves its inner world of stillness and self-containment.

Water is probably the most mysterious and least fathomable of the elements—so many-faceted, yet so potentially still and passive; so formless and adaptable—yet following laws of its own. It exhibits peculiar and apparently contradictory manifestations. As an example, its volume increases as it freezes. *Still waters run deep*—and the mysterious depths draw many curious probers.

Air

This is the element we all take for granted. Mostly we are not aware of air's refreshing breath or oppressing vapors unless we pay particular attention to its lightness, fleeting dispersion, permeability and inconstancy of direction in breeze or storm: This is air.

It strives away from the surface of the earth, expanding, laden with moisture or dry, as it vacillates between fire and water—no surface but all extension and expansion: This is air.

If the water content will permit, air offers us perfect penetration by eye as far as the horizon, with utmost clarity, colorless expanse and minimal resistance to motion as well as to our gaze, to pressure, and to form: This is air.

So patently open and invisible in its very permeability, so apparently predictable, and yet so constantly surprising in its modifications and endless variations of motion: This is air.

Air is an unpredictable ballerina—flitting from extreme to extreme like the weather itself, which resists all our attempts to cast it into stereotype patterns. Nay, it frees itself ever from the burden of form and shape. It escapes confinement in little amusing quirks and quavers, trills and sighs and breezes, or angrily roaring tempests sounding a mighty symphony of form-destroying power, until—in time—the air is cleared and again the tranquil blue sky helps us forget her very existence.

The Human Picture

The working of the elements gives us a starting point for our attempts to penetrate into the quintessence of meaning, which unites the world of humanity with the world of nature. Our observations of the dynamic working of the elements challenge us to form the concepts and images which may lead us from the world of nature into the inner world of an individual.

As Rudolf Steiner points out in *The Archangel Michael, His Mission and Ours* (Anthroposophic Press, Hudson, NY, 1994), human beings need again to learn to grasp hold of something which belongs simultaneously to nature as well as to the inner being of each individual. Through our head organization we have, since the fifteenth century, an incomplete understanding of nature; through our inner bodily organization we have an incomplete view of ourselves; ordinarily we fail thus to observe a process which works simultaneously within humanity and nature.

In speaking about temperament characteristics, Steiner points to one way of rebuilding a bridge—through our understanding—of the worlds of humanity and nature. It is, therefore, vital to grasp hold of the elements of nature and the human temperaments as two sides of the same nexus of dynamic forces.

Each element of nature works in individuals and reveals itself in a characteristic form of expression. This characteristic form or picture contains both psychological and physiological traits. Thus the element-temperament patterns of expressive form point to both outer—physical and physiological—as well as inner—psychological—facets. Human beings are thus revealed as partially separated from nature and partially united with her. They are united in as far as the physical natural forces work also upon the body; they are separated from her in as far as the physical natural forces are transmuted to serve as expressions of the soul while the individual impresses his or her essence upon the body. The relation of the human being with the created world has been a fundamental topic of philosophy.

At a crisis point of child development—approximately around the ninth year—this relation may be observed directly. Most children then undergo a change of their handwriting, often to the concern of teachers and parents. A caricature of the temperament characteristics of form and design seems to express itself then for weeks, or even months. An underlying profound psychological change is indicated by the shattering of the learned form elements of handwriting. As indicated below, working with the typical temperament forms in lettering styles helps exert a harmonizing influence on the child as well as giving him or her the tools to develop an individual style of writing.

The Melancholic

One day we may observe a slender person remaining shyly in the background of her group. She moves on the outside of the group, never in the center, as if anxious not to get too close to anyone else, thus preserving her independence. We may observe her thin, pale, slight body, hesitant gestures, delicate skin and silky hair. This person is withdrawn, tending to merge with the background, and cringing when circumstances focus attention on her. Not for her are sports and their excessive bodily involvement, nor the leading role amid her peers. It is the stillness she loves best, the quiet of a dark corner.

One day she may surprise us with a smile, sharing an observation or a thought which moves her, thus appealing to our understanding and compassion. Then we may also become aware that under her guise of passivity, her seeming listlessness, her apparent lack of interest, there lie sensitive perceptivity and great capacity for concern, power of observation, and compassion. Yet there is also excessive awareness of her own self, body and soul, which causes the melancholic to be so cautious in play and work.

Her awareness is centered upon herself. She relates all her experiences directly to herself and is therefore hypersensitive in this respect, but she has also the capacity of an excellent, detailed, and systematic power of memory.

If we were such a person—methodical, aware of form, hyper conscious of ourselves—we would take great care to protect ourselves. We would rarely reveal our inner selves, for we are suspicious of everyone around us. Being overly aware of ourselves, we lack self-confidence. Small handwriting, small drawings in a corner of the paper, dark colors—all we do tends to look as if we would like to solidify it, freeze it, mineralize it, compress it.

Of course, we may be hypochondriacs, too! Every little scratch and bruise is a great worry and concern.

Structure and order appeal to us and provide us with a much-needed framework for self-confidence. If our order is upset, or our expectations changed, we take a long time to adjust. In order to adapt to a new structure, a new subject, a new order, we need to be well warned and ahead of time. If not, the heavy burden of not being understood may cause us to weep silently into a pillow, to sulk in some dark corner hoping the cause of our hurt and pain will right itself without action on our part.

Slowness is natural to the melancholic, for in a world where all consequences are weighed up ponderously, rash, even fast, action, cannot be endured. This tendency towards immobility and inaction makes her pace too slow, too late compared to that of most individuals.

Confinement in attitude, coolness in manner, inactivity of the body—all this is on the surface of the earthy element in human beings. But let us not forget that within her there is the potential of crystal clear thinking, of a sharp memory, of dispassionate objectivity, and—last but not least—of abysmal loneliness.

The Choleric

Such an individual will be the first one to be noticed in any group. Probably a sturdy and compact fellow, he shouts, orders others around, instigates play and involves himself totally with action, making grand statements and grand demands. No shyness here, he is very well aware of his worth and in kingly fashion takes for granted any royal tribute offered him. Decisive as he is, determined to have his way, practical and often ingenious in action, nothing will deter him or thwart his clever and instinctive strategy unless an opposing will of equal power and determination comes into play.

Often bull-necked, broad-shouldered and big-chested, possibly of ruddy face and hair, he sports a direct gaze and a strong handshake. The choleric is a person of action, of involvement, of power, of hard work that really gets things moving. He knows just how to motivate others, too. Or, if mental powers are not equal to his innate energy, he may be frustrated and show much temper, often flaring and blazing into violence, for he would demand what he considers his right. There is great promise and potential in some cholerics when the most positive traits show themselves in originally conceived and superbly executed work. Conversely, there is also the capacity for destruction when he feels thwarted. Self-discipline becomes his great challenge.

The restless, impatient, expansive, dramatic, colorful mode of fire betrays itself in every move. Movement capacity is great. Sports that are challenging, that pit one against another in competition, are favored. The extreme choleric would like to take on the rest of the world, secure in the supreme self-confidence of his capabilities. To learn to control his extreme desires, and thus temper the sword of the mind in the fires of the soul, may indeed serve to forge the material of leadership and inspiration: This is the challenge facing the choleric. It is the challenge of transforming the destructive side of fire into the constructive one.

Guidance is also hard to accept for the choleric, for he sees it as limitation, which he abhors in any form. He needs to learn to control himself and to understand the social needs of others, lest overweening self-importance were to fan the fires of selfishness and loose forth a blaze of destruction.

Generous in deed and thought, to think big is natural to him. Every room is too small; even every sheet of paper is too small to contain the large works he intends to produce. Large gestures, big writing, and dramatic coloring—these tend to make him the center of attention.

His warm-hearted nature, his sense of humor, and his readiness for adventure—these make the choleric the pivot of any group. If there are others too much like him, fireworks are bound to be the result. But that expansive fiery nature will also allow him to see the necessity to overcome violence and use his fire rightly and thus develop true leadership qualities. It is sad to observe that too many cholerics fall by the wayside, their talents undeveloped, because no early tempering of the steel of their soul has given them a clear view of cause and ideals, and has thus left a wild sword in their hands.

If tempering, moderation, and self-control take root, then the choleric becomes the motivator of his group, the doer and the thinker, too, even the innovator and the inspirer: He becomes the man of rightful action.

Such is the transmuted fire element. Without it, the world would be a boring place, for cholerics bring as well as crave excitement in order to feed their inner flames. Enthusiasm is dispensed by them, and the great creative spirits of any age have given and partaken in this best of inner fires.

The Phlegmatic

Most of us have wondered about the seemingly ordinary child. Maybe he is a little more roundly built and lavishly upholstered than others. Maybe his remarks are more often directed to the commonplace events of the daily routine. Gossip about the ordinary things, about the little events of everyday life, is important to him. Ask him, though, about the big events, and likely as not he will not know or not remember. Does he or does he not know what you wish to find out? The surface ripples of ordinary events may just cover up what goes on in the depths of his soul.

The surface, the superficialities appear to be his bread of life. A comfortable exterior, a comfortable and easy-going manner as well as a real appreciation for all the comforts of life are evident in all he says and does. This is the phlegmatic. Like the waters of the world, his expression is fluctuating and diverse. He may be the chatty mountain stream talking his way down the mountain side, or the deep pond temporarily stagnant to the despair of all others who would attempt to get through to him, or sometimes even the wild ocean when, in some rare moment of frustration or misunderstanding, the deeps are stirred and the stormy outbreak reveals a glimpse of how deep still waters may run. Mostly, though, the picture of the stream is the appropriate one. The phlegmatic likes to conform, to be about average, to go with the crowd. There may be little brilliant insight, dramatic display of genius, or deep philosophical thought in him, but instead we find a dependable reliability distinguishing the phlegmatic to make him the backbone of society.

There is great need for routine and for the dependability of the physical side of life. If we wish to get something done reliably, a routine job, then the phlegmatic is the right person. His attitude to life, his imperturbability, shows itself in his tendency towards rounded forms, large and comfortable shapes, in bringing everything to one level, thus leveling off and filling out all available space, like water in a container. It is passive growth, in contrast to the activity of the choleric. The phlegmatic is down-to-earth, making realistic comments when we are expecting idealistic ones. We might make the mistake to think that he has only shallow emotions and superficial thoughts. We could very well be wrong, for—to reiterate—still waters run deep, and he protects his inner self well enough from our probing. When all others have exhausted their resources and have given up, he continues with compelling energy and resilient strength to turn the wheels of life on and on and on. Thus, routine is his strength.

Waters run downhill. So the phlegmatic will take the easy way whenever he can. But he will keep on going once he has begun. The fabric of society is kept together by all those who keep on going, doing their jobs.

The Sanguine

We all know the lively person. She is full of excitement, flitting from one sensation to the next like a butterfly, hardly pausing to take in one thing before going on to the next. She will crave constant excitement and will demand to be constantly amused. We are fond of her, however, as she is generally very likable. At times, though, her demands may become too irritating.

The sanguine is graceful and vivacious, maybe delicate, certainly pretty or well favored and often witty and light-hearted. She has a great need of changing impressions, as her quick mind and tongue delight in the titillations of eye and ear. She has—literally—all her wits about her.

She may also be the restless one, seemingly insatiable because ever dissatisfied, as she moves rapidly from one sensation to the next. There is always something bigger, better, grander, more fashionable, more exciting over the horizon. She collects and discards with ease, changing her views at the drop of a hat, defending today what she attacked yesterday. Constancy of expression, be it in motion, of conviction, or of character, is not natural for her, though over a period of time this tends to even out and balance.

She will do just as she pleases, for if her attention is taken by some remark, enticed by some sight, captivated by some sound, she will immediately act on it. She will thus plunge headlong into some course of action and find out halfway that she has not considered the consequences sufficiently and so winds up changing horses in mid-stream. Her detailed course will always be an irregular one. She will follow the spur of the moment; her life will run in little spurts and stops, irregular in detail but predictable and rhythmically repetitive in the long run. The rage of the moment, the man of the hour, the idol of the year, the fashion of the day—this will fascinate her and rule her life. And her innate charm and sunny nature, so candid and well-meaning, will ensure that one forgives her foibles, little inconsistencies, intrigues and manipulations, for is she not, when all is said and done, an innocent who cannot be held totally responsible for all that happens around her? She runs ahead of us one moment and behind us the next. Possibly she is inconsistent, uncaring, and enervatingly irritating, but all the same, gracious and charming about it; not entirely dependable, not totally irresponsible, but certainly full of dislike of being chained to any routine and regular work. If there are not enough dramas and intrigues in her life, she will probably invent them. Boredom is her greatest enemy, and a lot of her ingenuity is spent on how to keep the boredom at bay.

She shapes forms fleetingly—some would say superficially. Her skills are easily acquired but also easily forgotten, and paying attention to detail is just too boring. As long as she is still in the process of learning her skills, some careful work will be done and will often be harmonious and even beautiful, but a sustained effort in order to perfect further what she thinks she has mastered already is often too difficult.

Constant reassurance that she is wanted and loved is very necessary for the sanguine, or she will lose heart and never finish a project.

Obviously, she will be a good and amusing conversationalist. She has no hesitations to inform us of her innermost wishes, passions, desires and thoughts. Indeed, words are very much her medium, for with words she may gloss over any inadequacies in her performance, excite any listeners, and make things happen around her. Light, glitter, brilliant color, a breathtaking view, the promise of tomorrow—this is her life. All eyes, all ears, she will notice the smallest detail but forget it as easily.

Much of the dancing, smiling, innocent, light-filled airy but often irresponsible and inconsistent way of the sanguine lives in any child in this golden age of childhood.

Understanding Cosmos and Individual

> *Temperament is primarily a given thing. It is the form which the life of the soul has taken on, the basis of the bodily life. The body of the phlegmatic appears rounded and unformed, just as his soul's life is unformed. The forehead of the melancholic, his slender, often stooping form, his dragging steps are outward signs of the weight of his inner life; just as the light, well-made form and winged gait of the sanguine belong to his cheerful nature.*[2]

The characteristic expressions of a temperament do not only separate individuals from one another, they may also unite them. Moreover, the above description notwithstanding, both men and women may show any of the above temperament characteristics.

An outgoing nature is shared by both the sanguine and the choleric, although the latter will bring more power and substance to his actions, and make more sustained efforts. Both are warmhearted, open and direct.

The phlegmatic and the sanguine share a social disposition. Frequent encounters and zest for life bring people together, and weave the threads of life which link one person to another.

Thoughtfulness and coping with the weightier problems in life, as one penetrates the depths of existence, one passively in thought, and the other actively in deed—this links the attitude of choleric and melancholic as probers of the depths.

The possible arousal of great anger is common to choleric and phlegmatic. Excellent observation is possible to sanguine and melancholic alike.

Frequently, even usually, there is more than one temperament expressed within one person. Most human beings have a good share of all four. A very one-sided expression is rare. For the sake, though, of learning to distinguish between the four different temperament modalities, their working in the human psyche and the picture forms of nature, it is convenient and necessary to describe them as if one predominates. This is an important point to keep in mind throughout these pages.

If we are of fiery disposition, we respond to the fiery element in the world more readily than to the other elements. If we are airy the airiness of the world draws us, and likewise the earthiness and the wateriness. Thus like responds to like, and natural sympathy/empathy between processes, events, and facets of the surrounding world and our inner life become apparent to us.

In his lectures entitled *Mystery Knowledge and Mystery Centres* (Rudolf Steiner Press, London: GA 232), Steiner refers to this knowledge of the four elements as qualities of cosmic and human worlds as they were known in Greek times. He states that the Greeks had developed a sensitive faculty of discernment for these qualities in nature: Warmth gives rise to air and fire, cold to dryness and moisture. Steiner even describes the urge to experience the completeness of the four elemental qualities as a prime moving force in inspiring Alexander the Great to launch his campaigns of conquest.

In olden times, the working of that world which harbored the original forces manifesting these four qualities was known and experienced in very definite ways. It was generally clear—up to the end of the eighteenth century—that there is an intermediate, invisible world between the heavenly bodies and the earth, between the stars and humanity. The working of spiritual beings, God and the hierarchies, was experienced in the cosmos and from there it could work onto the earth. The elements had their home *sub luna*—in the sphere within the orbit of the moon. In *True and False Paths in Spiritual Investigation* (Rudolf Steiner Press, London, 1969, GA 243, Lecture of June 14, 1924), Steiner describes this intermediate world thus:

> *At all times this second world has been called the world of the elements . . . In the second world it is only meaningful to speak of the elements earth, water, air, fire and light and so on . . . Our senses therefore are rooted in the world of the elements where it is still meaningful to speak of earth, water, fire and air.*

Neo-platonic and hermetic writings up to the seventeenth century contain much mention of the elements and were known to every scholar worth his salt. One such sample will suffice:

> *But if all the four elements are combined together in fit proportions, then the creature is so made as to be ardent in action, light of movement . . . and solid in structure. For the earthy element is that which makes the body solid; the watery element is that in it which makes it diffuse itself so as to unite with things; the airy element is that in us which causes movement; and all these are roused to action by the fire in us.[3]*

The same forces work in human beings and nature in the form of the four qualities of the elemental world. It does not behoove us to return to the old conceptions, but rather to learn to understand the working of these forces in terms of modern humanity and appropriate to the modern world of the twentieth and twenty-first centuries.

According to Steiner, the transformational action of the formative-elemental forces is intimately involved with our digestive processes. Within these digestive processes our relation to the world of nature in the realm of substance takes place. In *Man as Symphony of the Creative Word* (Rudolf Steiner Press, London, 1970, GA 230), he states that everything of a mineral nature must be transformed into warmth ether, all plant nature needs to go through the transitional state of the airy, all animal substance must go through the transitional state of the water, and only that which is human may keep the earthy-solid state. This is one of the secrets of the human organism.

This seems to indicate that in our digestive processes we devolve all substances that we take in to their original evolutionary stage—the stage whence they came into being—thus, the mineral substance back to the warmth of ancient Saturn, the plant substance back to the air-light of ancient Sun, the animal substance back to the water of ancient Moon; only the human substance would be assimilated directly.[4]

This transformation in the realm of substance is our digestive process. In taking this particular process as an example, we become aware of the specific transformational activity of the elements, the etheric, or life, forces. Thus we follow the working of these etheric forces as agents of tranformation, as agents of life-giving processes active in the medium of time.

A particular temperament modality is, on the one hand, one of the peculiar patterns used by an individual when transforming into physical reality what lives in the soul as a form of thought, feeling or intentionality. On the other hand, one particular temperament modality shows the specific pattern by which the individual receives impressions of her or his environment and transforms them into the facets of the soul life. Thus the transformational action works in two directions—from the soul life outwards and from the sense world inwards.

Accordingly, we may call the four qualities—the fiery, the watery, the earthy, and the airy—the four major transformational agents. Their characteristics show us their particular patterns of transformation. The etheric world, the arena of life forces, is the home of both elements and temperaments. Or rather, one might say, it is the wellspring from which both come forth. It is the world of formative time processes. All is change and movement, firming and dissolving, evolving and devolving, in different tempo, mode and manner.

The teacher works with time. The right timing is of the essence. Temperament—*tempera mentis*—is the timing of the mind. We could also call it the seasons of the mind, maybe even the seasoning of the mind. As we delve deeper into the secrets of cosmos and humanity we become able to recognize the four essential qualitative modes of timing. We then learn to work creatively within the living web of time—as we should—when teaching.

The reality of the temperaments cannot be understood without their relation to time. They are basically rooted in the flow and the rhythm of time. That which is timing in music is temperament in man. A melody may sound quite different if its rhythm is changed from quick to slow. Its impression will vary with its tempo. The same sequence of tones when played at different speeds of rhythms will produce quite diverse reactions.[5]

Chapter Two

Temperament Language as the Key for Communication

The etheric body, as I have said, grasps by a tip what one calls the physical outer world. But what is ultimately the etheric body? The etheric body is ultimately what a human being receives from the cosmos, the macrocosm. So that since he detaches his etheric body from the macrocosmic condition the macrocosm lays hold of itself through his senses. We can feel ourselves as sons and daughters of the macrocosm—inasmuch as we are an etheric body and grasp the earthly sense-world with our macrocosmic part.[6]

— Rudolf Steiner

If we give ourselves up to meeting the marvels of the landscape around us we may have wonderfully vibrant encounters with majestic mountain ranges, stately rivers, lush forests, sweeping farmlands, lakes, clouds, beaches, and deserts. Our being receptive to the phenomena of the landscape enables them to speak to our soul. We listen to this language of forms and shapes and colors; their meaning is revealed to us directly, without the intermediate step of abstract and formulated thought. We know the nature of the landscape in its immediate impact as our sentient body streams out and grasps forms and colors and textures with its variegated senses. Steiner describes the sentient body as that part of our soul perceptible to our senses, which is in continuous interaction with the world around us.

The form language of the mountains, the foothills, the lake and the ocean is archetypal. It requires no explanation—seeing is knowing. Words are unnecessary—for the formative forces in the landscape speak to us directly. This is the gestalt—the gesture—of the landscape. Equally so each tree, each shrub and flower, each animal, each human being has his or her typical gesture, which we read and from which we derive instant and direct knowledge, though most of the time below the level of our conscious mind.

What is Temperament Language?

In earlier centuries, this form of direct and instant knowing was called reading in the book of nature, and it was a way to the mysteries. Then, sudden insights in the open mystery of the book of nature could lead an individual to the deeper mysteries of the essence of humanity and the cosmos. The goddess Natura would reveal herself to those who studied her with loving attention and devotion.

> *During sleep, however, human beings experience their union with the cosmos, with the super-earthly cosmos, just as during waking hours they experience the common life with the earthly cosmos by means of their senses. When what they experience in sleep becomes visible to an individual, in that moment he stands before what was until about the thirteenth century called Nature. The sleep experiences of human beings were called Nature, and what the Middle Ages called Nature was called by the Greeks Persephone, Proserpine.*[7]

Today, our very sense perception has dulled, and we have acquired the bad habit of the age of materialism to ignore matter and attempt to *look behind the scenes* for the physical forces, molecules and atoms, thus degrading nature and by implication declaring her to be a sham and illusion.

How different was the relationship of a human being with nature in distant ages. Regarding the language that human beings spoke in those primeval times, Steiner expresses in a lecture on *The Recovery of the Living Source of Speech*:

> *So that in those older times we find words that express how human souls react, what they find themselves impelled to do under the influence of the world around them. The most ancient language of all consisted almost entirely of expressions of will.*[8]

One may gain the impression that the ancient will language, given to humanity through the archangels' intuitive perception of the workings of the second hierarchy of angelic beings, was predominantly one of gesture. Throughout all Steiner's works we may find an abundance of indica-

tions linking the human experience of world and society with the existence, striving and activities of angelic beings. He uses the hierarchic order
of angels, as first mentioned in the Christian traditions of the early medi-
eval centuries, in describing them. He also indicates repeatedly how these
hierarchic orders correspond to spiritual beings in non-Christian religious
and mythological depictions.

In a wonderful description of a Lemurian scene—a group of men
gathered around a priestess—Steiner speaks of the relation of the ancient
human beings to nature:

> *Those around her move in rhythmic dances. For this was
> the other way in which* soul *entered into humankind. The
> mysterious rhythms, which one had heard from Nature, were
> imitated by the movements of the limbs. One thereby felt at
> one with nature and with the powers acting in her.*[9]

Humanity and nature spoke the same language of gesture, of
rhythm and of song. It was the language of the elements, which was heard
and spoken by human beings.

In the lecture on *The Recovery of the Living Source of Speech*, mentioned on the previous page, Steiner characterizes the development of language further into post-Atlantean times. The archangels in the course of
their own evolution now enter into a relationship of being inspired by the
beings of the first hierarchy. This enables them to bestow on humanity a
language of feeling.

> *Language itself is metamorphosed. Words become an expres-
> sion before all else of sympathy and antipathy, of every shade
> of human feeling. Instead of a language of will, as in former
> times, we have now a language of feeling.*[10]

Later the ethnic element in language became the predominant
one. The purest temperament expression is to be found in the modulation of the timing of any process. Language flows differently when words
are spoken in a fiery, an earthy, a watery, or an airy manner. The stress on
the musicality and time modulation of rhythm in language inspired the
creation of long epics. Indeed, archetypal rivers of language were flowing
from paradise in all the cardinal directions of the earth.

Concurrently with the development of language we must take the development of memory as described by Steiner, for instance in his lectures on *World History in the Light of Anthroposophy*.[11] Rhythmical memory and language of feeling are connected. Temperament qualities now enter into the pure timing process. They become more inward in human beings.

The third step in the development of language occurs with the archangels turning—again due to their own evolution—to the past of the earth to form imaginations, through which they endow humanity with a language of thought. The word-thought-picture memory also develops concurrently from the end of Greek times on.[12] Certain implications for our own age arise out of this development of language.

> *And inasmuch as speech now took its source from an earlier stage, into it crept an Ahrimanic element. This is a fact of incalculable significance. And what the Archangels felt above them came to expression in the world of human souls in a deadening of speech and language. Language became polished and at the same time paralyzed; it no longer retained the livingness it had in earlier days.*[13]

In our century we witness an ever-growing mechanization in the handling of language. We may observe in the pre-schooler the child who still speaks a language of will and gesture. Thus our own body motions, our actions, even our intentions—as yet unmanifest—speak to her or him louder than words. The child knows us, and the world, directly through our body language.

The elementary school child speaks the language of feeling until around the twelfth year. It is particularly important for her that we address her in the language of the temperaments, because the most direct correspondence of language and temperament lies in the rhythmic-feeling area of language.

It should be obvious that the "dead language of abstraction" is a necessary field to conquer and master for the high school student. Temperament imagery and quality are no longer found, and rightly so, in abstract language.

What, then, is the language of the temperaments? When speaking, we intend to communicate a body of meaning. This meaning may be expressed in gesture, shape, or event: It may be expressed in actual words; it may be put into a picture; or it may be put into dramatic sequence of an event—either a naturalistically accurate or symbolical image, an allegory, or a metaphor. A body of meaning can be expressed as gestalt; it can be expressed in a fiery, an earthy, a watery, or an airy mode of form. Whenever it is clothed in words, these words may be uttered in a fiery, an earthy, an airy, a watery tempo and manner. The musicality inherent in language may thus also take on temperament modulations and change its tempo and intonation accordingly. Even the very sounds may contain consonants related to the fiery, the watery, the earthy or the airy element.[14]

The formative forces of the elements may be of help to find the appropriate form of pictures and images. As teachers, we have to find the relationship between contents and element-temperament characteristics if we intend to find the appropriate picture. After all, images and pictures contain components of sensory perception, but in this particular case, freed from direct perception by the power of the mind. When tracing the origins of a meaning to be expressed, we may find the corresponding element of nature, and thus arrive at images and pictures which are not contrived, but inherently logical and thus appropriate.

I must make a remark here about the difference between contrived and inherently logical work in the field of artistic-creative expression, for we work artistically when forming pictures. As an artist, one might have today—and did have in earlier ages—an instinctive knowledge of the etheric form principles through one's relationship to nature. Much of modern art shows the loss of this instinctive knowledge of the formative principles, and so may become a caricature and distortion of what the natural principles of form actually are. Today, this knowledge has to be regained by consciously directed and deliberate work. As a Waldorf teacher, one has to find methods by which to awaken the forces of the soul—slumbering in every person—which are connected to the creative form principles in the natural world. As the four elements show distinct and characteristic form principles which are reflected in the temperament modulation on the human level, working with these principles—in other words, applying temperament language—will engender creative-artistic potentials in our students. Then we are in a position to *teach* creativity. These pages are intended to show a way for the teacher to awaken creative impulses in child or adult with the help of his or her anthroposophical insight.

The essence of temperament language in its three modifications emerges now clearly: form/gestalt, tempo/rhythm/sound, image/color/picture. We restore depth and fullness to language by using gesture, sound, picture, timing, rhythm, and image in meaningful concordance with each other. By doing this, we rebuild the foundations of experience; we go right to will and feeling by using the four elemental qualities in modifying and enriching our threefold forms of expression.

LANGUAGE OF THOUGH — IMAGE COLOR PICTURE

LANGUAGE OF FEELING — TEMPO RHYTHM SOUND

LANGUAGE OF WILL — FORM GESTALT GESTURE

One Example

In telling a story describing the cow, we may use slow, flowing gestures, an even, probably slightly monotone voice, unexciting, factual words. We ourselves might sway slightly in rhythmic motion, as if we were in the process of becoming watery—for a cow is a most phlegmatic animal. If we do this, we clothe the abstract meaning of the words with the corresponding living sensory qualities, which enter the child's soul directly instead of detouring via the intellect. Thus we build a bridge of knowing and understanding with immediate impact.

The watery element—the phlegmatic temperament—will feel strongly addressed by the above description. It will recognize and sympathize with the facets in the description that are similar to itself—same recognizes same—and, via the bridge of assimilating the similar, will also be able to take in the dissimilar parts of the description of the cow. Moreover, the listener will have the experience of truly understanding on other levels than only the intellectual, and the speaker will have the experience of being truly understood. Thus by using the temperament imagery of corresponding sensory qualities, we build bridges of understanding.

Another Example

We describe the flight of a bee. It flies an obviously erratic course, dashes around us, hovers, and settles maybe. Over a period of time, a pattern will be seen to emerge: the bee works her way towards a particular direction in a winding and circling path. Our very speech will become bee-like. So we shall express the airiness, the sanguinity of the insect again on all levels of language in gesture/motion, in tempo/sound/image, provided we steep ourselves in the character of a bee. By using our own faculty for acting, for choosing descriptive words, modulating our pitch and tempo of speech, we endow our language again with the life which, due to modern intellectual tendencies, is in danger of being lost to the human being. Moreover, by using the languages of will and feeling in their various modalities, which precede the intellectual language of thought in our time, we speak appropriately to the child's own state of development.

Let us stress again the following: Each person has all four temperaments active within her or him, just as each person's bodily nature is subject to the working of all four elements of nature. A very slight preponderance suffices for one or the other temperament to predominate and endow us with a characteristically individual modulation of expression. Indeed, we are able to apply the imagery of the four qualitative elemental forces effectively, precisely because they are at work in each person.

After all, the knowledge of the four temperaments should not tempt us to adopt the attitude that this person is such and such because he has such and such a temperament! That would be a subtle form of fatalism. Nor should we be tempted to use that knowledge to indulge in a subtle form of *behavior modification.* No one has the moral right to *modify* another person's behavior. If change of behavior is necessary, this needs to be recognized and done by the person her- or himself. We may, however, provide the opportunity and setting which enable others, particularly children, to change themselves. But if a person exhibits one-sided temperament traits, then our own knowledge of the particular quality will enable us to establish channels of communication with this person more easily.

If we have presented the elements and the temperaments in strong relief, it is only for the purpose of characterization, not because we ought to remain with a rigidly conceived differentiation in the reality of the weaving of life. Both in nature and in each individual there is a working together of all the four qualities—of this we must be aware—so that we are able to use them in fullness in our teaching approach and, in general, in communication with our fellow human beings.

Rudolf Steiner's Examples of Temperament Teaching

Steiner used three main subject areas in order to demonstrate to the first teachers of the first Waldorf school in Stuttgart, Germany as well as to his listeners in other parts of Europe, how knowledge of the temperaments may be applied concretely in teaching. He worked with the teachers on the art of storytelling, incorporating the temperament modulation. He gave detailed examples of drawing exercises in connection with temperament characteristics, showing how transformational processes typical of particular temperaments arise in progressive metamorphoses of forms. He demonstrated the practical use of temperament work in the introduction of the four basic operations in mathematics to first graders.

In the art of storytelling, we are almost purely concerned with enlivening the musicality of language itself—tempo, sound characteristics, and suitable word pictures. Drawing exercises take place in the area of gestalt metamorphosis. In mathematics we deal with four possible relationship patterns as expressed in the typical temperament picture. Instead of emphasizing the end result of the arithmetical computation as the essential factor, the process is stressed. There are four different processes—four different modes of time. The arithmetical problem is made fluid and so expanded into a process in time.

Is it coincidence that Steiner chose his three main examples of temperament teaching in these areas—gesture, process, language—thus correlating it with the unfolding of the three stages of language development in humanity? Or was his intention, by giving these examples, to point out that temperament work should pervade all three areas, the acting/gesturing/moving, the feeling/timing/procedural, as well as the imaginative/conceptualization area of the child's learning experience?

Needless to say, Steiner gave examples, as he did in all other areas of art and science, in order to show paths of research, paths of developing and applying the gifts of anthroposophical knowledge that he transmitted. At no time did he intend that we should remain rigidly with his examples, because in time the totality of teaching practice is capable of being permeated by anthroposophical ideas. This thought should encourage all teachers to find their own ways of enlivening the subject matter by permeating it with temperament language. Before we go into more examples of how this may be done, we need to focus yet more extensively on the key process involved.

The Key Picture of the Learning Process

Steiner appealed to the teachers of the first Waldorf school to permeate themselves so strongly with the power of imagination that they would be able to recreate the subject matter anew every time. This power of imagination enlivens and stirs up the interest of the child, and also our own interest, in the subjects to be taught.

We need to awaken within ourselves the sources of inspiration; this enables us to re-create the subject matter. Let us be clear about our task. As teachers, we should treat the subject matter in such a way that we make it palatable for listeners—child or adult—season and spice it just right according to the age group so that it becomes nourishment and is digestible for the listener's soul. We are really alchemists—or cooks, if you prefer—who tread the pathways of the four elements of nature, when recreating the subject matter.

The key factor is that we must do the hard work of analyzing each component of the subject matter so that we track down the working of the four temperament qualities. Then we can portray them in gesture, speech, and image.

Analysis is not easy. It means to find the fundamental phenomenon, to hunt for the fundamental sensory perception and immediacy of soul experience, and cast out the garbage of preconceived ideas, of prejudiced conclusions, of half-baked popular scientific concepts. We must have the courage to stand apart from the tide of technologization of knowledge, of definition and rigidity, and turn with each component of knowledge, with each step in the acquisition of a skill, again to the original and archetypal phenomenon. We must have the courage to go in search of the origins of each area and body of meaning.

Further, we must have the courage to find, see, and work with the triune aspect of cosmos and humanity. Then we may find that interwoven with the threefoldness is the fourfold quality of the elements of nature. But at the back of the fourfoldness is a threefoldness. The basic polarity of the elements is the polarity between the contracting and expanding forces. This is modified into the four. There was a time on earth when water and air were intermingled—only three elemental qualities were then active in nature.

We may realize, moreover, that here is a natural progression of the learning process, beginning with the will aspect of a subject matter, progressing to its feeling aspect, and finally culminating in the forming of its conceptual contents.

In *Foundations of Human Experience* Steiner describes how to wake up a child's thinking by letting him or her walk and speak simultaneously. [15] By activating a child's body movements, that child's thinking is eventually stimulated. This simple indication, if applied diligently, is, in truth, a magic formula for education. Steiner describes further that our ego—by which he means our eternal self— enters the world of pictures and images of the external world and is awake in them. (Steiner's view of the self is decidedly not Freudian; therefore the ego in Steiner's usage is not an expression of our lower drives and instincts, but the spiritual entity, which is an eternal, spiritual being.) Thus is the ego able to take hold of cognitive thinking. Each step accompanied by a spoken word is a spur to the ego to wake up.

We mentioned above that the human soul experiences in sleep the world of nature. From this world of nature she awakens to her day of wakefulness and consciousness. If we strengthen the experience of the world of nature rightly, naturally, and emphatically, by using temperament language, we lay an appropriate foundation for the picture forming activity of the waking consciousness.

Through the correlation of direct observation and anthroposophical insight, we may know that the child should first experience and act out the inherent elemental gesture contained in new material to be learned. Then he should transform the bodily-spatial-gesture-motion experience into the timing-procedure-rhythm experience, and finally contract the latter into an inner picture in the realm of thought. This sequence is the key for internalization in relation to the learning process. Temperament language is an essential factor at each stage.

Therefore it is of paramount importance to permeate all that is done and experienced in the classroom with the four qualities. Just as the working of the formative forces in nature is continuous and does not stop, but follows its own inherent logic of evolution and devolution, so we need to create the four temperament qualities constantly throughout our whole teaching activity, allowing the life stream of the temperaments to permeate all teaching. At times, changes in tempo will suffice to infuse a different quality into the classroom. At other times, we need to become actors, impersonating the fiery, watery, airy, earthy elements. The subtle combinations of gesture, timing, and imaging are the keys to speaking temperament language. This approach requires a phenomenological manner of approaching our environment. How can the teacher learn this? Steiner referred to this problem in connection with his lectures entitled *The Boundaries of Natural Science*:

> *We are now in the right frame of mind to guide our souls in the direction briefly indicated yesterday—along the first steps of the way leading to Imagination. It is possible to pursue this path in a form consonant with Western life if we simply try to surrender ourselves completely to the world of outer phenomena, so that we absorb them without thinking about them.*
>
> *If we thus bring our activity of perception into a state of flux, as it were, and infuse it with life and movement, not in the way we follow when forming concepts, but by working on our perception in an artistic or symbolizing manner, we shall develop much sooner the power of allowing the percepts to permeate us in their pure essence. Simply to train ourselves rigorously in what I have called phenomenalism— that is, in elaborating the phenomena—is an excellent preparation for this kind of cognition.*[16]

Thus if we, as teachers, cultivate the habit to allow the sensory phenomena to impress themselves upon us undiluted by preconceived thought, we shall allow our faculty of perception to flow, much in the same way that this happens in perception related to symbolizing or artistic activity and so engender a feeling for the phenomena. In cultivating the purity of the sensory perception, we develop at the same time sensitivity for the four distinctive qualities of the elements permeating all natural phenomena. We then sense the hidden fire, water, air, and earth in nature and become able, gradually, to recreate subject matter artistically, feelingly, imaginatively, and livingly in the classroom. Only then will our teaching answer the demands of our time.

KEY PICTURE

LANGUAGE OF THOUGHT	IMAGE COLOR PICTURE
STAGE THREE	
LANGUAGE OF FEELING	TEMPO RHYTHM SOUND
STAGE TWO	
LANGUAGE OF THE WILL	FORM GESTALT GESTURE
STAGE ONE	

Stage One: We and the child move and gesture in fiery, earthy, watery, and airy modes, expressing a context of meaning.

Stage Two: The child and we modulate speech, live in the sound/rhythm/tempo expressive of that same context of meaning.

Stage Three: We and the child clothe concepts arising from the same context of meaning with sensory qualities corresponding to the four elements.

The pathway of a context of meaning from the language of will through the language of feeling to the language of thought indicates the transformation of experience into knowledge in a manner innate and appropriate to human beings, and thus to the child.

The Re-Creation of the Subject Matter
An Example: Introduction to Geography

Steiner in his work with the first teachers of the first Waldorf school, gave examples of applying temperament teaching in three areas (as described above). I shall give an example of temperament teaching, but not in the area of storytelling, form drawing or arithmetic, as Steiner did. It should be noted that the following example describes in condensed form actual work that I did with one of my classes. This could be an example of the teacher's preparation of the experiential activity of her class and is not intended to set a rigid method. The aim of this subject is the introduction to the hometown surroundings as a preparatory step to geography proper. The starting point is with the spatial experience of the child.[17]

In order to know where one should begin in the introduction of a subject, one should be clear what the specific psychological situation of children in that particular age group is, in respect to the subject. The time of the ninth-tenth year of life is of particular importance in regard to geography.

As a brief preamble I shall describe one way to depict child development as understood in Steiner's philosophy of the spiritual human being. Children have lived during infancy and early childhood with their intentionality, their experience, and their sensory perception more acutely and sensitively within their surrounding than within themselves. Their nexus of formative forces is still in the process of contracting the residue of past incarnations' ego experiences into the shaping and forming of the physical body. One might picture the ego (the self) penetrating children from the head downwards since birth, and, also, penetrating from the surrounding inwards. Let us remember that in the spiritual world, before birth, the human soul has been poured out, as it were, over the widths of cosmic space, and in preparation for incarnation, the individual has been contracting, contracting, until finally arriving at the physical body. Once born as an earth being, the human soul then has the reverse relation to the surroundings to that which she or he had in the spiritual world—now experiencing the self as the center and looking out into the surroundings. The changeover from cosmic to earthly orientation, begun at birth, is completed around the ninth year. Children then become conscious of themselves as separate entities. Any psychological crisis, described at various occasions by Steiner when discussing the developmental stages of childhood and youth, is a reflection of the fact that a child's self wakes up at this point, this lonely center. It is now confronted with having to look out into the surrounding world, which now appears alien to the human soul, having lived in it instinctively when younger. However, from this time on, the human soul begins to extend awareness of the world from within outwards. This process of growing outwards, this conquering of the dimensions of space from the center out, is very important for an individual's subsequent capacity of finding the appropriate place in the world and the relation to humanity as a whole.

In introducing geography we have third and fourth grade children before us who are at this crucial turning point of spatial experience. They are ready to wake up in the *geographical space*—not bodily of course, but mentally, with their imaging capacity.

I have here attempted to put down the steps I took in this introduction to geography. This example shows one way to make alive to students an entity of meaning by using intensive temperament modulations.

Step One

The child arrives with his or her awareness of being in the center, so we must begin where the child is—in the center with the child's physical body. We let him or her look about, note what may be seen in different directions, make her or him aware that landmarks are always in the same location. We discuss the location of the sunrise, of the sunset, and begin to differentiate the spatial sphere around.

Take the four cardinal points of space. Let students attempt to find for themselves North, East, West, and South. Characterize differences by discussion—cold, warm, sunrise, sunset, and any other, such as seawards and landwards, for example.

Then we begin a structured activity: The children stand in the center of the room, close their eyes and attempt to execute commands: "Take three steps South, one step North, hop four times to the West," and so forth. This would be repeated daily over several days, after which time a natural feeling for the different compass points usually awakens in most children.

By varying this activity subtly in several ways—changing tempo or tone of voice when giving instructions—we bring the temperament dynamics to bear on this experience of the children.

We may differentiate further. We may speed up the change sanguinely when stepping East or slow down melancholically when stepping to the North. We may glide along phlegmatically towards the West or stride cholerically towards the South.

Step Two

Now we discuss what we would be able to observe if we were to hover high above the school building and see into the classroom. We locate other landmarks, roads, rivers, and so on. We test the students' feeling for direction by asking them to point in the direction of the various landmarks. Instead of getting them to move toward the compass points, we might say: "Take three steps towards X road, four steps towards Y mountain, one giant leap towards Z river, but don't fall in! Tiptoe toward M city." In this way we differentiate further the child's conscious sense for space. We would engage the class in this type of activity for several days, until we notice a growing awareness of orientations. Our *journeys* become, of course, ever more complex and exciting.

It is important for the teacher to realize that this activity of combining bodily movements with an imagined mental picture is vital for the next step, putting down on paper what we have enacted in person. We may make a drawing of the four compass points, or even the more differentiated one of the wind rose.

Guess which colors we are going to use for the four cardinal points. That is a test for us to establish an inherently logical picture right down to the details of choosing the appropriate colors. An individual's relation to the four cardinal directions is neither incidental nor accidental—colors have been assigned to the cardinal directions in many cultures, such as Native American, Maya, Chinese, and so forth.

We then delight the children by working out the names of the in-between directions, for at this age factual detail is relished. Then we can remind the class of the bird's eye view of the immediate surrounding, and ask each child to draw, as best she or he can, the surroundings from above. Thus the first simple map comes about.

Step Three

Now we need to go beyond the horizon. We go on imaginary journeys. What do we meet when going South, East, West, North?
In discussion and by reporting in graphic detail what lies beyond the horizon, we build up a picture of what we would meet. Only then are we ready for activity—structured and varied according to temperament characteristics.

The activity could be like this: We group the whole class in the center of the room. We orient ourselves, say by facing South. We speak, walk, and mime as we begin our journey:

"We go South" (three forceful steps).

"We cross the Z River" (on the name of the river, we walk in a wavy line with our feet, and make wave movements with our arms—we are now depicting water).

"We see farms, corn fields, barns, silos, a railroad track" (we point to each in rapid succession, sanguinely and in lively manner; we also trip lightly).

"We come to the Y Mountain" (arms are held up high, stiffly, we are now earthy, contracted, melancholic).

"We arrive at M city" (we walk strongly, asserting ourselves in the city, indicating the massive buildings with our hands—cholerically).

The whole group chants, mimes, steps together. We explore the world. We repeat this for a few days every day until the class has assimilated it. Bodily actions are now fused firmly with imaginative descriptions.

As it is vital that children know what they are doing, they should accompany each action by speaking appropriate sentences; or, after having practiced these imaginative journeys for some days, repeat them silently for themselves, and thus raise the whole experience yet another notch towards the conceptual, which must be our aim after all.

A reminder: It is our task as Waldorf teachers to lead children to form concepts in such a manner that as adults the further step—imaginative knowledge—becomes possible if the individual, out of free choice, decides to work at developing his or her spiritual potential.

Step Four

We are now ready to draw what we have acted out before. We draw as exact a representation of our choreographed journey as is possible. We thus raise up our experience from the will experience of the body via the language-feeling area into the image area.

Our drawing could look like this:

It goes without saying that colors and forms must correspond to the nature of the object we portray if we wish to achieve our purpose in integrating the different levels of experience. Color-coding is of the essence. Thus mountains would probably be violet or blue, look hard and tall, contracted—our very writing becomes like a mountain range, with the single letters as the peaks. So we follow the inherent logic of nature, and arrive at forms and colors consistent with the workings of the nature forces: We are thus actively continuing the work of nature. The above example—showing letters like mountain ranges in their appropriate color—also shows us how to avoid fantastically contrived shapes, which lack inherent logic.

Step Five

After a few weeks, there are now several journeys going on at the same time—one is being acted out; another being drawn on paper; maybe a third is acted out silently and invisibly in the mind. The internal picturing capacity should now be stimulated sufficiently in each child so that he or she can repeat mentally the details of a journey. It is vital that we take care to complete the threefold process and allow the child to work on the mental level as a third step and not cut off the process before the last level is reached. After all, one aim we pursue as Waldorf teachers is to lay the foundation for qualitative thinking. With this we have raised a body of meaning—such as the journey South originating in our own locality—from the physical movement activity to the artistic-visual-formative activity of drawing or painting, and on to the mental level. Outer experience has become inner picture through these stages of transformation.

Step Six: Conclusion

We have now extended the child's awareness in all cardinal directions. The students are now firmly anchored in a cross formed of all four spatial directions.

Each lesson now contains the choreographed motion of making a journey, a drawing-feeling-picturing activity, and the mental recapitulation which stimulates the child's inner picturing skills.

It should become clear in this example how the use of the four temperament/element qualities is subtly interwoven at every step and has helped in forming the transition from the one area of activity to the other, from engaging one part of the human organism to another.

We could expand further the children's spatial awareness by discussing relative positions of important places in the surroundings, thus gradually building up their skills for judging relative distances and preparing future map reading skills.

It is obvious that we may draw on a number of artistic media in order to enliven the process which leads to geographical knowledge: Acting, moving and miming, forming plastically—we may also model the landscape—drawing, painting, reciting, and even singing. In short, a wide range of artistic expression may be used.

The teachers needs to prepare by analyzing the subject matter, getting as far as the fundamental phenomena, but not breaking through them into the abstract, fantastic or contrived. Then they may express the subject matter in all three forms of language and meet the students where they really are.

PART TWO

TEMPERAMENT CHARACTERISTICS
IN THE REALM OF ARTISTIC EXPRESSION

Chapter Three

The Arts and the Senses

*A path to art must be found that will link once again the
sphere of the spiritual with the sphere of natural science.*[18]
— Rudolf Steiner

Each art form uses elements of sensory perception. If we are to
understand the essence of art, we need to understand also that which lives
in nature. Rudolf Steiner continues,

> *I must now add that it appears to infer in the conditions of
> modern civilization that we shall only find the right path to
> art when we have first explored the right path in relation to
> the investigation of natural phenomena, the path of spiri-
> tual science. For in the sphere of art today mankind is so far
> removed from building the bridge of which I have spoken
> that it can only be persuaded of the active permeation of art
> by the spirit when it can be finally convinced of the activity
> of the spiritual that can be seen especially in the genesis of
> the pathological; when there is clear evidence of how the
> spirit operates and reveals itself in matter. When mankind
> becomes aware of the activity of the spiritual in the king-
> dom of nature, then it may perhaps be possible to arouse
> sufficient whole-hearted enthusiasm for the idea that the
> spiritual can be presented directly to the world in the form
> of works of art.*[19]

One major challenge to modern humanity can be described as the need to reconcile the demands of a lucid consciousness for thinking with the usually submerged area of the instincts and the semi-submerged area of dreams within an individual's psyche. We may detect two aberrations of art in our century which arise from this challenge: one, wild abandon to the instinctive and the emotional expression, because the guiding light of thinking is denied any part in the artistic process, and two, premeditated and contrived expressions which use artistic media to express a construct of thought coldly and devoid of feeling. In neither approach can we find a truly human spirit as expressed by great art.

At this point something needs to be stated, which may cause surprise when mentioned in an educational context. Education has the task to help young souls develop the potential to accomplish their aims in life. It is apparent that many internal and external forces and influences in today's world pose grave obstacles to the balanced development of an individual. It is further apparent that there is a great longing in many people to find a spiritual source of strength. Humanity has crossed the threshold into a new age of light, as is often stated in Eastern beliefs. This age of light was to come after five thousand years of a dark age, specifically in the year 1899. The inertia of nineteenth century materialism, however, continues this age of darkness and still builds ever more monstrous juggernauts of technology in order to ensnare human minds. Steiner, too, spoke often of the end of the age of darkness and the beginning of an age of light. Individuals experience a split in their souls between the residues of the dark age and the promises of the new light age even more acutely now, than was the case at the beginning of the twentieth century. From a cultural viewpoint, art is uniquely suited to be a healer of this split—in the individual as well as in society at large.

The question of how to develop artistic impulses in children which lead neither to the mystically-voluptuous nor the trivially-contrived, but instead towards the humanly balanced—which may be seen as the universally Christian—ought to be in the heart of everyone who hopes to help develop education as a healing impulse for humanity. The term *universally Christian* is used here to characterize the moral-ethical foundation of Christianity devoid of any attachment to a particular church, creed, or denomination. In this sense Steiner indicates repeatedly the importance of Christ for the totality of human evolution and His significance for individuals, quite apart from their specific religious beliefs.

Art as Expression of an Individual's Essential Inner Forces

Steiner elucidates the relation between the different arts and the inner human being most profoundly in his lectures on *Art in the Light of Mystery Wisdom.*[20] He states that the forms of artistic expression arise from the fact that the forces of one member of a human being's inner organization—such as the etheric or the astral body—are, as it were, pushed into the realm of the next lower member and become active on this lower level. He gives the following diagram:

Members of the Human Being's Inner Organization

Life Spirit	Arts
Spirit Self	Eurythmy (Dance)
Eternal Self – Ego	Poetry
Astral (or star) Body	Music
Etheric (or life) Body	Painting
Physical body Sculpture	
	Architecture

Regarding the members of the human essence, an in-depth overview is given by Steiner, for instance, in his book *Theosophy, an Introduction to the Spiritual Processes in Human Life and in the Cosmos* (Anthroposophic Press, Hudson, NY, 1994, GA 9).

In the case of architecture the forces of the physical body are separated entirely from a person. Thus, architecture stands by itself as a monument of human creativity in the mineral realm of the earth. Sculpture comes about through the work of the etheric—or life—forces in the realm of the physical body; painting through astral—or star—forces working into the realm of the etheric; music through ego forces pushing into the astral realm; poetry through the inspiration of the spirit self—which is still outside us to a large extent, and has not been brought as yet to individualized expression except in a few and remarkable individuals, and thus enters from the future—working in the realm of the ego; and eurythmy—which is still in its very infancy as a particular form of dance—as intuition of the forces of the life spirit working into the spirit self.

It is beyond the scope of this book to examine these far-reaching indications of Steiner here as deeply as they deserve. But we should come to a bacis understanding of the implications of the above diagram from the viewpoint of the developing young person.

Architecture appears to be the oldest art of mankind, its beginning lost in the shrouds of history. It would be fascinating to examine the styles of architecture from the viewpoint of the polarities as described in the first part of this book. Although the architectural forms which surround us influence us profoundly, we shall refrain from concerning ourselves here with their effects.

Sculpture—apparently the second oldest art of humanity—will have to be dealt with here differently than in a work on art in general. The growing child—through her or his etheric body—still expends life-formative forces on the growth of the physical body. These forces are therefore very much in a state of flux. It is my personal conviction, gained by observation of children, that for the growing child a delicate approach to all sculpting activity is vital. If we encourage plastic expression too strongly, in my view, we harm the proper health of the growing child. The formative forces should really only be called upon strongly after puberty. The medium which we use before that age is thus significant: cold clay, which is rich in calcium, should be avoided: it sucks the etheric forces too strongly out of the child and into the clay. Warmth-endowed beeswax is really a much more appropriate medium up to the tenth year. The avoidance of clay until the tenth year is particularly important for the Western Hemisphere, where the formative forces create solid structure very easily.

The child—whose own physical form is not yet fixed—lives in flowing movements, which are on the way to becoming firmly established. Instead of sculpture and the full use of the plastic arts with the elementary school child, we could speak of plastic and movement arts together as one area of artistic expression. Further, painting, music, and language arts will show that in the young person a different relationship exists between the members of his being than in the adult.

I shall not consider eurythmy in these pages other than a brief mention, for much has been done and established in this field. From the viewpoint of the above diagram, though, it should be clear that I do not mean eurythmy when speaking of movement art in these pages.

Contraction and Expansion in the Realm of Art

The challenge which the great cosmic powers of contraction and expansion hurl at an individual's ability to hold a balance also extends to the realm of artistic activity and expression. The very spectrum of the arts reflects these polarities as stated by Steiner in the above-mentioned book on the *True and False Paths in Spiritual Investigation.*

By and large, the arts are under the domain of the Luciferic beings. However, architecture and sculpture are more influenced by the Ahrimanic formative and contractive beings. Music and poetry are particularly influenced by the luciferic beings. It is of the essence, though, to be clear that geographic cultural-ethnic influences modify this general scheme. Moreover, Steiner warns, it is entirely possible that also luciferic influences work into architectural and sculptural styles and ahrimanic impulses can penetrate very easily the realm of music—as they do forcibly in much of contemporary music.

Painting represents a balance between these two polarities. Not a static balance, however, but a dynamic one, because here the attacks of the two contending powers are particularly vicious, so that succumbing to either influence is easy. Great energy and determination have to be found by an individual who would withstand the one-sidedness of these polar opposite powers in order to create the balance in painting.

Before discussing, in some detail, the fields of experience of several of the arts in relation to teaching, we need to concern ourselves with sensory perception in relation to the arts, to the temperaments, to the inner, human being, and thus also to the two cosmic powers of Lucifer and Ahriman. Steiner speaks repeatedly and with great earnestness of two great spirit powers whose intent it is to tear apart individuals into their physical-physiological and psychological-spiritual halves. Social groups, in all forms, ranging from a class to a political party or a nation, are also affected by their activities. It is too simplistic to refer to these powers as the embodiments of impractical idealism in the case of Lucifer and self-promoting materialism in the case of Ahriman, but this simplistic description might give us a handle on beginning to understand their effects on human beings.

Individuals and Their Senses

> *The real aesthetic conduct of man consists of the fact that
> the sense organs become enlivened, as it were, and the life
> processes become ensouled.*[21]

This statement gives us a more definite indication of how to direct our work such that the beings of the major arts may be resuscitated
from their sleep, into which the cold intellect of the evil fairy has cast
them. The necessary paths for the awakening of the senses as hinted at
above require us to turn to the phenomena of nature. The above quotation leads us further, for we should understand that the enlivening of the
sphere of the senses and the ensouling of the sphere of the life processes in
individuals result in aesthetic appreciation and activity.

What does this mean? Steiner states that our aesthetic activity
based on a feeling for beauty comes about because the astral body of the
head comes into play with the astral body of the rest of our bodily organization.[22] (Astral forces activate our consciousness and our physical movement. Their configuration in each individual is the astral body.)

An actual realignment takes place in our inner organization whenever we are engaged in making aesthetic judgments. We are dealing here
with a correspondence and relationship between physiological and psychological aspects of our inner being. The astral body of the head and of
the rest of the body holds a dialogue—the contractive forces of the head
converse with the expansive forces of the rest of the body. Moreover, we
may consider the enlivening of the senses and the ensoulment of the life
processes also in connection with the transformation of the consciousness
soul into the spirit self. That means that in the same measure, as the consciousness soul receives sense perceptions of the physical world, the transformed consciousness soul—that is, the spirit self—receives sense perceptions from the world above the world of thoughts. (Steiner's description
of the consciousness soul as part of our inner configuration may be found,
as mentioned above, in his fundamental book *Theosophy.*)

In such a way art prepares the path for supersensible perception.
The senses are like gulfs of the physical world reaching into each human
being and engaging there all members in turn. A person's sentient body,
the oldest yet least conscious part of the astral body, reaches out into the
surroundings and actually touches, as it were, the astral counterpart of the

objects in the physical world. The fact of this contact is brought to our attention in sense perception. The outward astral movement runs in the counter direction to the physical motion and, in the case of sense perception, sets up complex waves of reflexes in our astral body—in either the head part or the body part. Physically the objects of the outer world seem to impinge upon us; astrally our awareness sends out astral feelers to contact these very objects. Probably for this reason Steiner states that each conscious sense perception is accompanied by other—minor—perceptions, to which we normally do not pay sufficient attention.

> But the senses also differ from one another in a further respect: some of them afford a relation to the outer world that is experienced more as external nexus; the others more one that is bound up very intimately with our own being. Senses that are most intimately bound up with our own being are (for example) the sense of equilibrium, the sense of motion, the sense of life—and also of course the sense of touch. When there is perception by these senses of the outer world, it is always obscurely accompanied by experience of the percipient's own being. You can even say that in their case a certain obtuseness of conscious percipience obtains, precisely because the element in it of external relationship is shouted down by the experience of our own being. For instance: a physical object is seen, and at the same time the sense of equilibrium furnishes an impression. What is seen is sharply perceived. This 'seen' leads to representation of a physical object. The experience through the sense of equilibrium remains, qua perception, dull and obtuse; but it comes to life in the judgment: 'That which is seen exists', or 'There is a thing seen.' Hence, in the whole gamut of the 'senses' there are some that mediate relation to the outer world rather less and the experience of one's own being rather more.[23]

With each impression that enters through the gates of our senses, complex vibrations occur and sound through the totality of our being much like the overtones accompanying each musical tone. As the typical quality of sound which differentiates one musical instrument from another is determined through the particular combination of overtones, so—

I would propose—is each major sensory perception accompanied by the harmonics of minor ones.

I would suggest that in artistically activated sense perception the consequence of the enlivening of the senses is that the minor sense perceptions begin to resonate and vibrate more strongly than in ordinary perception. Maybe one could also say that they become slightly conscious, in a dream-like way.

Thus one major sense is emphasized, but if it is a body sense, it needs the harmonics in the spirit and soul senses; if it is a spirit sense it needs the resonance in the body senses and vice versa. We have thus a stronger and *musically* activated interplay between the three groups of senses.

It is necessary to point out here that Steiner speaks of twelve senses, seven more than the traditional five. In recent years several senses have been added by research, notably the body senses of equilibrium and movement. The spirit senses have so far been neglected by main stream psychology. If one assumes their existence as a hypothesis, pedagogical practice seems to prove their independent existence. The small child, for instance, appears to have a sense for the units of sound composing a word before understanding its conceptual content, thus showing a division of sound body and content of word. The senses of word and thought reflect this differentiation. For instance, important research in this field was done by Noam Chomsky, which he describes in his *Language and Mind* (Harcourt Brace Jovanovich, Inc., New York: 1972).

Body Senses	Soul Senses	Spirit Senses
Equilibrium	Warmth	Ego
Movement	Sight	Thought
Life	Taste	Word
Touch	Smell	Hearing

Here we need to remind ourselves that a differentiation process takes place in the head—Ahriman is active there. The unifying process takes place more strongly in the body—Lucifer is active there. Thus with the head senses—the spiritual senses—we reach out more towards spiritual perception. As our ego and astral body are more loosely connected to our physical head organization, the possibility for greater objectivity, as well as for fragmentation and differentiation, is enhanced there.

With the body senses, the unifying processes take place because in our body ego, astral body and etheric forces are more directly and inwardly engaged in organic processes. With the middle senses, equilibrium may be noticed. In these soul senses we mix objective and subjective experiences. Steiner describes the role played by Lucifer in regard to the body senses and Ahriman in regard to the spirit senses thus: A constant dialogue goes on in the realm of the senses between the unifying body senses—touch, life, motion, equilibrium—and the differentiating spirit senses—hearing, word, thought, ego—mediated by the soul senses—smell, taste, sight and warmth.[24]

If we understand which senses participate within each art form we have the possibility to enliven that art by taking care to work also with the minor senses and not only with the main sense perception which forms the vehicle for the respective art. Temperaments serve as agents to help bring about the enlivening of the senses and the ensoulment of the life processes.

Senses, Elements and Temperaments

Steiner speaks in various ways about the twelve senses of human beings. As the senses are not our main topic, I shall refrain from attempting to reconcile some of the apparent contradictions in many of his statements but will instead approach them from the viewpoint of the temperament-element modalities.

> We only have to become accustomed to the idea that the treatment of the senses must not be limited to describing them according to their more obvious organs, but that we must analyze them according to their fields of experience.[25]

Let us then concern ourselves with the quality of earthiness. This relates to the earthiness in ourselves and in our surroundings in a threefold way: At the first instance, we knock against solid objects occasionally and at times rudely, and then becomes sharply aware of ourselves as well as of the texture of the foreign object against which we knock. At the second instance, we may receive into ourselves minute particles of a solid nature from the outside which convey to us the essence of other objects. These experiences of essence often touch us emotionally. At the third instance, we may become aware of the inner structure and state of being of an object through the sound it makes when struck. In all three instances we are concerned with an experience connected with the earthy element and its formative principles.

Our first experience is a totally subjective one—we become aware of our own body by having tactile sensations. The second is part subjective, part objective as we smell the essences of other objects and recognize them by their typical aromas. In the third instance we hear whether an object has a perfect or an imperfect form by the very sound it makes when set to resound. Its form, shape and structure reveal themselves through sound. The sense of touch, the sense of smell and also the sense of hearing are thus related to the earthy element and its formative principles.

Earthy Quality: Touch   Smell   Hearing

Let us consider the essence of fluidity/liquidity. We can imagine that we could follow the dissolving and coagulating activity of our own inner, bodily, life processes as they surround, or stream in and out of, our inner organs like a stream around an island. This flowing differentiation confirms us in our sense of well being if all is well and alarms us if obstructions arise in the inner order. This is the most subjective experience. Mostly we do not pay much attention to it except when we experience sharp pain and discomfort. We can equally direct this quality of inquisitive flowingness towards substances entering our organism from the outside. Then we taste whether they are fit or unfit, whether they agree with us or not. We are both subjective and objective in this field. The formative forces behind the fluid, mercurial state help us discern the different taste sensations and with it also divine their effect on us. Thirdly, we may detect the modulation, the whorls, quavers and vortices as they form and dissolve as liquid organs in yet another stream—the stream of speech. This enables us to experience directly—and this is objectifiable—the single sound units that form a word. Each word we hear and understand is one of these vortices in the stream of language.

Here we have three levels of experiencing liquidity: entirely within ourselves as the sense of life; within the foreign substance as it enters us— the sense of taste–and objectively, as we hear the flowing stream of speech when listening to others, the capacity to differentiate between single words.

Watery Quality: Life   Taste   Word

Let us turn to the airy quality: We may direct our inner mobility—the word "direct" does not necessarily imply a conscious process—towards adjusting, balancing and juxtaposing the movements and postures of our own body, its limbs to each other and to motions determined from the outside. Secondly, we can detect an inherent movement in the colors of objects around us as they approach or recede from the plane of vision, and consequently take on different hues. Thirdly, we may hold on to a purely spiritual movement and grasp the fleeting thought as it flashes in our consciousness, as it meets us from the outside, from our fellow human beings.

The sense of movement links us subjectively to our own body and so to our physical surrounding; the sense of sight conveys the emotional movement of colors as they approach and recede within the space created by the formative forces of air and light; the sense of thought enables us to direct our consciousness, to accompany and understand the thoughts of others in their swift flight.

Airy Quality: Movement   Sight   Thought

Let us consider the fiery quality: Firstly, we establish an independence from our surroundings by overcoming the three spatial directions; we proclaim our independent existence in establishing our own equilibrium within space. Secondly, we continuously equalize our inner blood heat with the temperature of our environment. We thus establish our own warmth body, which is influenced by and is in interaction with but independent of the warmth of our surroundings, under normal climatic conditions. Within this warmth body we are free to transmute physical warmth into soul warmth, physical cold into soul coldness, as the case may be. Here the border between physical and soul substance is thin indeed. Thirdly, we can be aware of our head as the quiet and still center of our body and experience our wholeness thus within. This feeling of ourselves as a wholeness of form serves us in recognizing the presence of other *selves* in human society.

On all three levels of the warmth-fire experience we have to deal with a transmutation and conquest of the given so that our own essence may become established. Space is conquered through the activity of the sense of equilibrium, emotion through our sense of warmth and we recognize the spiritual essence of human selfhood in others through our sense of self.

The sense of equilibrium asserts our own bodily self against our physical surroundings so that we can stride freely over the earth and imprint in it our own selves through our actions. The sense of warmth makes us independent from our surrounding so that we may send soul-filled warmth or cold into it and become active and creative in the field of the emotions. Through our sense of self, our sense of ego attributes, we have an objective experience of the form of human beings which houses a human individual. These are the three levels of warmth experience.

Fiery Quality: Equilibrium   Warmth   Self

In this way we may relate our twelve senses from level of the bodily subjective to that of the spiritually objective. Steiner calls these three levels of sensory experience the body senses, the soul senses, and the spirit senses. It is essential to realize that in each group a four-fold aspect of elemental formative forces comes to expression.

East and West—Upper and Lower Human Being—the Senses

Steiner also states that the six lower senses are the basis of modern Western culture and the higher six the basis of Oriental culture.[26] As this seems to be in contradiction to our description, we shall examine this statement more closely.

Earth	Water	Air	Fire
Touch	Life	Movement	Equilibrium
Smell	Taste		

We find here that the contractive elements predominate: earth and water. The contractive elements within this group of six senses are, as it were, squeezed out, filled with subjectivity, externalized, and filled with matter by Western humanity in the process of technologization which began several centuries ago. We may be reminded here of Steiner's remark regarding the origins of the idea of atoms in modern science: A modern scientist speaks only of atoms because he projects his own nervous system into the world.[27]

Let us look at the other six senses:

Earth	Water	Air	Fire
Hearing	Word	Sight	Warmth
		Thought	Selfhood

Here the expansive elements predominate. These six senses are the basis of the Oriental cultures, notably the ancient cultures. Religious mysticism dwells much in the experience of these senses, clamoring for unification, for the overcoming of egotism. The denial of individualism which is implied by this emphasis on unification with others and world is an illusion of sacrifice that can be engendered by religions and ideologies.

Let us clarify these statements. When the contractive forces work at the periphery, from the outside in, and the expansive forces from the inside out, we get a high degree of interpenetration. One could say that then—or there—a person is incarnated, and integrated, strongly. Such a person acts individualistically and is much concerned with him-or herself. When—and where—the expansive forces work towards the outside, and the contractive forces towards the center, then the degree of interpenetration is minimal and the incarnation is loose and slight. Such a person is not too concerned with the world of nature, indeed is often indifferent to it.

In the region of the body senses we tend to be too strongly incarnated; in the region of the spirit senses we are too loosely incarnated. Our individual East is in the head region; our individual West is in the metabolic and limb region of our physiology. The middle senses are the mediators. They tend to be used too little in the East. They tend to be under too great an attack in the West.

The balance between the Eastern and Western hemispheres of the earth, the head and limbs of the individual human, depends upon the healthy state of the middle senses—the senses that link us with the world spread out around us in the circumference.

Correlation of Senses and Elements in the Individual

SPIRIT SENSES

Hearing   Word   Thought   Ego

SOUL SENSES

Smell   Taste   Sight   Warmth

BODY SENSES

Touch   Life   Motion   Equilibrium

EARTH   WATER   AIR   FIRE

For, take the scientific spirit that emerged, the scientific spirit that tries to apply mathematics to everything. Mathematics, as I explained to you yesterday, comes from the senses of movement and balance. Thus even the most spiritual things discovered by modern science come from the lower man. But modern scientists work above all with the sense of touch.[28]

Further, a present-day danger is that the health of the middle senses—smell, taste, sight and warmth—is undermined by the use of and addiction to fake and illusory sense perceptions. Artificially derived scents and flavors, on the one hand, and television, cinema and fake warmth in the form of electrical heating on the other hand, both subvert the capacity for a sound judgment of sensory values. This upsets a person's ability to hold the balance with the surrounding world. These effects show themselves in widespread incarnation disorders, consequently also in learning disorders. It is obvious now why these disorders would show themselves more strongly and disastrously in Western humanity.

Steiner once made a surprising statement that the following was foreseen by Christian Rosenkreutz and other highly developed individuals: In the future mankind could develop into two completely different types, who would have little understanding for each other. There would be men concerned only with the material aspects of life, with all that technology brings about. Then there would be others concerned only with spiritual aspects, shunning involvement with the material side of life. There would be no way this split of humanity could be prevented. Help could only be brought about if human souls were to be educated in spiritual worlds before birth.[29]

We may also state that help can be brought about if individuals learn to participate in the life of the cosmos again, in the life of the planetary spheres of our solar system. Then the individual may be able to balance—through the gates of the middle senses—the one-sidedness of head or limbs, East or West in him- of herself, and through their own state of balance influence beneficially the world around.

Arts, Senses and Elements

Each art needs the foundation of several types of sense perceptions, as already indicated above. Artistic experience and expression bridge the gulf between the two hemispheres, between upper and lower human being, and so between the polarities of Lucifer and Ahriman.

Painting works with the airy triad—the senses of movement, sight and thought—but is anchored down, as it were, by the sense of taste. The pigment is put onto the surface through the motion of the brush stroke. Our sense of sight helps us decide which hues to choose and where to place them—to weigh them up in tone and composition. Our sense of thought may detect meaning expressed as image. Our sense of taste agrees or disagrees with adjoining color hues, as well as with the whole painting. This is a result of the enlivening of the senses. Painting works from the astral into the etheric nature of man—from the airy into the watery: Thus the air senses predominate and the water senses resonate.

Sculpture works with the watery triad of the senses of life, taste and word, and is anchored down by the earth senses. It works from the etheric into the physical, from water into the earth. Our hands form the medium through flowing motion—isolating, damming up or thinning respective sections of the work. Taste balances the parts of the composition. Word brings an entity of feeling-emotion alive into tangible form, and gesture, and so anchors it down.

Architecture is working with the earthly triad of touch, smell and hearing, and is anchored down, a strange expression in this case, maybe centered would be better by the sense of ego. It works from the inner, the physical, into the outer ego. When architects make models of their buildings in clay, for instance, they engage their tactile sense. Smell differentiates and balances. Hearing allows spaces and structure to be in harmony. If a design is artistically balanced, the acoustics in a building are also sound. The sense of ego tells one whether there is a wholeness of design and purpose. Earth is predominant here but is sounded through by fire. Whenever we leave behind us in the world tangible traces of our ego activity in the earth, we bind our ego-fire nature into the earthly.

Music works from the fiery triad—equilibrium, warmth, and ego—into the earthy triad: touch, smell, and hearing. The fire senses predominate and the earth senses resonate. It is a reversal of architecture.

The first Goetheanum at Dornach was conceived musically and for this reason its architecture, sculpture and painting met with so little understanding. And for the same reason, the second Goetheanum will also meet with little understanding because the element of music must be introduced into painting, sculpture and architecture, in accordance with man's future evolution.[30]

Poetry works through the airy triad—motion, sight and thought—into the watery triad—life, taste and word. The sense of equilibrium also plays a role in anchoring it down, as Steiner points out. The sensitive and fickle mobility of air is reflected, harmonized and rhythmically bound by water.

Eurythmy works from the fiery triad into the airy one. Fleeting forms, fired through with enthusiasm, are inscribed into a fleeting medium of air.

The above suggestions are of course only one of many possible interpretations. We have here a working together of different sensory facets and processes in order to enliven the fields of experience in each of the major realms of art. In this way contractive and expansive forces, physical head and limb being, *Eastern* and *Western* senses, converse with each other whenever the human soul is engaged in artistic experience or activity.

In each art form most of the four elements are active, however differently proportioned. Some senses predominate, others harmonize and resonate. Each temperament may find a way to each art through the element-sensory experience. The major sense of life, for instance in the art of sculpture, will speak to the phlegmatic. However, the minor echoing senses of touch, hearing, and smell will speak to the melancholic in a kind of ground swell. Thus by being involved in each art—through the interplay of two or more element-sensory qualities—we promote the balancing and harmonizing of the temperaments in the human beings.

In this chapter we have given some beginnings of potentially major research into the relationships between senses, temperaments and different forms of art. Readers are challenged to develop their own examples further.

Chapter Four

Movement and the Plastic Arts

*Just as in architecture we push the laws of the physical body
into the space outside us, so in sculpture we push the laws of
the etheric body one step downwards. We do not separate
these laws from ourselves; we push them directly into our
own form. Just as we find in architecture the expression of
the laws of our own physical body, so we find in sculpture
the natural laws of our etheric body; we simply transfer this
inner order into our works of sculpture.*

*So if we seek the laws of sculpture we must realize that they
are in fact the laws of our etheric body, just as the laws of
architecture are to be seen in the laws of our physical body.*[31]
— Rudolf Steiner

There is a children's game called "statues," which is well-
known in many countries and on many continents. It goes like this:

*A group of children run around an open space, haphazardly
and as they please. One child—by prearrangement—calls a
sudden halt. The most interesting or exciting posture—
termed statue—which comes about by freezing the position
of one's body as the halt is called, is judged to be the winner.
This game, in its instinctive wisdom, shows the exact relationship of the child under ten years of age to the plastic
forces.*

Movement Arts—Pre-Sculptural Arts

The etheric/life forces are continually in mercurially rhythmic
motion of expanding and contracting, firming and dissolving. They take
hold of the fabric of matter to give it firm or mobile shape as needed. The
forms of the world of nature are the result of their activity.

The etheric/plastic/life forces in the young child work almost exclusively in order to establish the physical body, crowning their foremost

formative work by causing the eruption of the permanent teeth. Thus we may conclude that though these forces establish the permanent and stable *forms* of life in the kingdoms of nature, their *activity* shows perpetual and diverse motion. Form may be said to be a consequence of motion.

> *You can either stare at something beautiful or you can experience the beauty in it. Today it is a fact that most people only stare. When this is the case it is not likely that the etheric body will be roused. By staring at something beautiful we do not experience it. But the moment there is an experience of beauty there will be a stirring in the etheric body.*[32]

We may perceive actively or passively. Perceiving passively—staring—leaves our soul being cool—it does not involve us. Perceiving actively means that we allow our own soul to be stirred. We may also say that in perceiving actively we begin to focus on that which is in permanent mobile activity behind the stable forms of our surroundings. In other words, when perceiving actively the phenomena of our environment, we look beyond the stable form upon the prior activity which had created this form. We thus enliven our own perception.

As the growing child applies her or his plastic forces mainly to the forming of the physical body itself, it would be contrary to an education based on knowledge of the human being to divert too many of these forces into plastic activity apart from the physical body at too early an age. But—turning again to the process of the game "statues"—we may strengthen the child's plastic forces by strengthening the stage before the more static and stable form arises, namely the mobile and dynamic stage of movement.

One is reminded here of a story about the Jesus child in one of the Apocryphal Gospels. It is told that, when Jesus was four years old, he bade the floodwaters of a summer storm to gather and be clear of mud, then scooped up the mud and formed two sparrows of it in life size. Being scolded, for this happened on the Sabbath, he commanded the sparrows to fly up into the air, which they did.

After the tenth year, however, and increasingly so after puberty, we need to engage the plastic forces as they express themselves in the formation of an inner architecture of thought, of logically constructed as well as plastically sculpted forms. In both areas the young person reaches beyond the bounds of the physical body. The capacity for reaching beyond the body and shaping the world outside thus needs to be supported and strengthened in adolescence.

For this reason, I regard movement activity as a prior stage to plastic activity. Obviously not every kind of movement is a pre-sculptural movement activity. Both the art of Eurythmy and the practice of Spatial Dynamics, as new forms of movement, inspired by Steiner, have developed into disciplines whose practitioners have worked for years at mastering their arts and are diplomaed from their particular schools. I do not discuss these two special forms of professional discipline when speaking of movement activity at large. In these pages, I hope to establish that movement activity outside of these disciplines may be developed as a dramatization of the subject matter, requiring carefully worked out choreography that demonstrates the content and essence of a subject. There are especially two areas of directed and constructive movement activity, which I shall attempt to describe.

Spatial Movement Arts

What we need to consider here are the movement arts available and necessary to the Waldorf teacher who is not trained in either discipline. The following remarks are probably particularly useful to the class teacher, as he or she carries the greatest responsibility for the long-range education of the child.

The two movement arts not generally recognized as such are the following: one is commonly regarded as a branch of another art form, though Steiner indicates strongly that this is not so. The other is more easily recognized as a movement art proper. The first is linear drawing on a two-dimensional plane. The second may be called the dramatization of subject matter in a choreographed, and spatially enacted, sequence of events.

Choreographed Dramatization of Subject Matter

In the example of the introduction to geography in Chapter 2 we have given one instance of how to choreograph and direct such an experiential learning experience, as the concepts of spatial location, relative position and landscape characteristics become enacted and portrayed by a group of students.

We shall consider here another example, namely an introduction to the four mathematical processes: addition, subtraction, multiplication, and division. Before doing so, some general remarks regarding such dramatizations are needed.

In standing still and upright, all three dimensions of space surround us. In walking, we move over the horizontal plane of the earth. The left-right dimension is also exercised, because we shift our weight from left to right and back as we walk. We are still upright and so relate actively to all three dimensions when walking.

Steiner points out that it is not immaterial which spatial plane we use in the course of an action. He relates the following, when describing the space experience of an individual in olden times.

> *In experiencing the above and below he felt weaving in the universe all that today we call the intelligence, the reasoning of the universe. All that rules in the universe as intelligence was interwoven in space with his idea of the above and below, and since he could share in this intelligence of the world through his growth from below upwards, man felt himself to be intelligent. The participation in the above and below was at the same time a participation in cosmic intelligence. And participation in the right and left, in the interweaving of sense and shape, of wisdom and form, was for him the feeling that weaves through the world. And his restful remaining still, surveying the world, was to him a uniting of his own feeling with the universal feeling. His striding through space in the direction of forwards or back was the unfolding of his will, the placing of himself, with his own will, into the universe, the universal will. He felt his own life to be interwoven with the above and below, the right and left, the before and behind.*[33]

All those familiar with eurythmy and Spatial Dynamics will know how much the living experience of space is fostered by these two arts. For the class teacher also it is of crucial importance to create the possibility for the students to inscribe—through their own actions—the essence of the subject matter into three-dimensional space. This activity of inscribing translates the subject to be learned into the language of gesture/gestalt, the primordial language of will as characterized above. It might be pointed out at this point that the young child experiences space in a different way than an adolescent or an adult, because it is still in process of being formed by the cosmic processes which impinge upon it from all directions of space. Young children live naturally in an ocean of movement and learn eventually to conquer this space and make it their own. By using movement in the initial stage of a learning experience, this experience is deepened immeasurably and becomes eventually part of an individual's conceptual capacities.

If we move in a left-right direction, that is laterally, we move over towards the form element to the right and the wisdom element to the left (This is not the place to discuss the phenomenon of the enormous increase of left-handed people in recent decades, though the reader is encouraged to reflect upon this fact in relation to the above statement.)

If we move in the forward-backward, that is in the sagittal direction, we move in the direction of firming or dissolving matter. What is before us is physically perceptible; what is behind us is hidden from our eyes. To step backwards into the matter dissolving—but spirit-revealing—stream without looking takes courage! But to step forwards all the time, and exclusively, means moving in the direction of constant consolidation of material existence. This is one reason for Steiner's repeated admonitions to teachers to encourage children to do things in reverse sequence, such as reciting the multiplication tables or walking and speaking sentences forwards and reversed. To do things in reverse order strengthens the self—the self is after all a spiritual, not a material entity.

Finally, the vertical direction relates a human being to the polarity of the earthly-cosmic, to the forces of consciousness and the unconscious within him. The head is the seat of consciousness; the body the seat of instinctive and unconscious events.

The basic form for the starting point of any group activity is very often the circle. The circle—an archetypal form—contains many a social secret, not alone because it gives the opportunity to develop social harmony without the danger of any one individual being dominant. The circle, however, only comes into tangible existence when all who are in the circle move along its circumference. The moment all stand still, we are left with an abstraction of the circle, for then the living ring falls apart in as many fragments as the number of participating individuals. Therefore the starting moment is a circle created by movement.

A class standing quietly in a circle is a hair's breadth away from the moment of creation. The circumference of the circle is an equilibrium, out of which we move and into which we are to be gathered again after completing the movement at hand. This is not a book relating specifically to pre-school children, though it might be pointed out here that the way in which pre-schoolers are able—or not—to move with others in a circle when playing circle games is a fairly accurate measure of their level of social interaction and maturity.

Example: The Four Mathematical Processes

It must be understood that the following presents but one way how these processes can be made a living experience to first graders. Before describing such a possible activity, let us say one word about orientation in the classroom. The child should move in the classroom in such a way, that the floor becomes, as it were, the paper, or the board. Movements should be oriented and correspond to the same directions of up/down, and left/right, as they would be were he or she to work on paper at the desk or to view the board. We confuse the child's sense of direction, instead of developing it, if we do not take care to align carefully the orientation of the required activity.

Moreover, when working with intensive choreographed movement activities as the experiential part of the learning process, the first element is an imaginative content, a story, which the students may picture inwardly and live themselves into the situation, which the story describes. Such stories for the introduction to the four processes in grade one are an essential component and furnish the material for the experience of the process. The typical content of such a story, of course, depends on the typical experience of children in the area—stories dealing with farming or gardening are easily adapted to number stories. I personally feel that stories dealing with imaginary elementals and their jewels (as is one Waldorf tradition) are best left in the realm of the imaginative, but when dealing with math we, after all, wish to introduce students to the quantitative aspect of actual objects. Through mathematical processes we develop cognitive capacities and hone them to a factor of precision and learn to develop focus for our mental processes.

One more comment: I feel that the four processes belong together as a group, as they depict four different types of social interactions between human beings and objects, which may be easily translated into temperament modalities. Consequently, I personally have always worked with all four operations in the same lesson.

Addition

The Story: Assuming that we tell the story of a market gardener preparing produce to take to the farmers market, we could begin by describing the harvesting of, say, heads of cabbage. These are collected in baskets, then loaded onto the truck, and driven to market, where they are displayed. During the collection process we have the opportunity to say, "There are 15 cabbages in the basket; John brought 6, Mary brought 5, and Cesar brought 4."

The Enactment: John selects 6 children, Mary selects 5, and Cesar selects 4, who go (run more likely) to a corner of the classroom designated as the basket. Eventually they are laid out on the farmer's stall in the market place. While this takes place, the whole class accompanies the action by speaking: "We are now 15; there were 6, then came 5, and then came another 4." An illustration of this event is made, and eventually, out of the drawing, the right notation of a number sentence is developed. We choose our verbal phrasing very carefully, so that it is suitable to be translated into the right sequence for notation. The action of lining up different quantities is a phlegmatic one.

ADDITION   SUBTRACTION

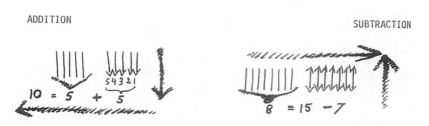

Subtraction

The Story: Now that the produce is set out at the market, there are buyers. Melanie buys 3 cabbages, Victor buys 7 cabbages, and George buys 4.

The Enactment: "1 cabbage is left; first 3 were bought, then 7, and finally another 4." This is the text of the verbal accompaniment to the *going away* of the 14 cabbages. As above, an illustration showing the process easily depicts the experience. As we prepare to write the number sentence as caption for the illustration, we always note first the end result of the process, that is, in this case, the answer of the computation. The activity of *taking away* can definitely be experienced as a melancholic one.

Steiner remarks that the teacher should notate problems by writing the answer first—that is the factual result of the process. The end result is mentioned first, and therefore we have to show on the other side of the equation the process which has brought about this result. When introducing equations in grade seven we can again dramatize them. I have done this with good results. Of course, we have here again a demonstration of the qualitative differences between the right and left side of an equation: On the one side is the fixed form of the result—the answer. On the other side the wisdom-filled process. Both result and process complement each other to become a totality. Steiner remarks that if mathematics had been taught from a spiritual view point—that is from the viewpoint of the totality—then it would not have been possible for communism to come about.[34] What is a totality? In regard to mathematics, I feel, one can take the present actuality for the totality. We need to take note of the actuality first and proceed from there to its parts. The stages of the process in any computation which have brought about the present actuality are then as parts to the whole.

Multiplication

The Story: The story of the selling of the cabbages could also take another form—we could describe the cabbages being lined up on the sales table in 5 rows of 3 cabbages each.

The Enactment: 5 rows of 3 cabbages each show us the actuality of 15, but now ordered into equal groups. The accompanying words might be, "We are 15: we are 5 rows of 3 cabbages each." Again the actual amount is named first, and then the process is described. We can delight the students in a very sanguine activity by having the 15 cabbages *tumble* out of the basket and sort themselves into the 5 rows of 3 each rapidly, and several times. With an activity like this we have a wonderful demonstration of the delight shown by sanguines when sensationally swift changes of size and direction take place.

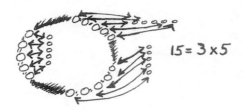

$$15 = 3 \times 5$$

Division

The Story: Division is a more complex process. When introduced in first grade for the first time, it might be good to consider *sharing* instead of *dividing*. The sales process could be as follows. The 15 cabbages are laid out on the sales table. 4 individuals come to ask for an equal number of cabbages.

The Enactment: The farmer now becomes the *divider*—he or she, one by one, gives out one cabbage in turn to each of the 4 buyers. This is possible 3 times, and then only 3 are left over. Division is truly connected with the ego because there is always one actor needed who is selfless—the divisor—to do the actual sharing. (This individual does not claim anything for him- or herself, but fulfils a social task impartially and kindly—a moral role.) Because of this, the farmer—the *leader* and divider—embodies a choleric action.

Naturally, the motions accompanied by the appropriate words are repeated over and over again, for several weeks, with different numbers. Finally, the actual process of each type of arithmetical relationship becomes well known to each child. Needless to say, notation follows the choreography of the movement action. These are but scant indications of how it is possible to experience the spatial dimensions livingly and create the mobile processes which precede the fixed form. The creative illustrations by the students complete the process and help establish the final conceptualization of the four processes.

Here is a side remark about using the fingers for counting. The formative forces sculpt the *five-ness* of the human hand. This is a fixed factor. Moreover, the hand does not represent a whole, but a part of the human body. I have found that I have held up, instead of helped along, the learning of number manipulations when encouraging the use of the fingers before working with each child itself representing a whole unit within the social group. Counting with fingers is already the second step in number manipulation. The first is the spatial re-enactment of a mathematical process by a group, in which each individual child stands for a whole unit—for one—because the four processes represent truly four different forms of social interactions.

Some readers may find it presumptuous that I use the term movement arts for the above description of teaching arithmetic. The teacher, though, in a dramatization of number processes, is a conductor coordinating the various elements of the process with the living fabric of a group of people; he or she is an artist working with the fluid medium of a group, expressing four possible ways of interaction in the four processes.

Steiner describes in detail how each temperament is related to each arithmetical process and how the reverse calculation is related then to the opposite temperament.[35] Generally speaking, the temperaments color each process in the following manner: Addition is mainly for the phlegmatics, when starting with the sum total; subtraction is mainly for the melancholics, when starting with the remainder; multiplication is for the sanguines, when starting with the whole also; and division is mainly for the cholerics, when working from the quotient to the dividend. Needless to say, all children, regardless of their temperamental tendency, need to be able to work with all arithmetical processes. These temperament indications are thus very important in the initial introduction to the four processes. Inasmuch as each individual needs to learn to develop all four temperament responses, she or he also needs to learn to manipulate all four processes.

Drawing—A Movement Art

If we continue the trend of thought which began by stating that facts—having become—need to be dissolved into the processes by which they became, we might arrive at the following realization: Patterns emerge as the residual traces of motions. For this reason I state here that some forms of drawing actually belong to the movement arts and not to the visual arts.

Steiner states repeatedly that a representational drawing with *outlines* is actually a lie, for the shape of an object appears to us visually through the difference of color and light, on its sides and planes, not by virtue of any actual lines. The line has no substantive value and should not be used in a visual representation.

As a track of movement, though, the line has reality and objective existence, even if it only portrays what is already past, for the respective movement has taken place before. The line is but the residue of a motion, just as much as my footprints in the sand or snow remain as a visible residue of my walk.

Of course, there exists a type of drawing that does belong to the visual arts. I offer the following remarks because I have seen instances in the practice of Waldorf education where the two types of drawing were mixed up with each other, thus bastardizing both arts. Linear patterns, geometrical patterns and figures, as well as writing, are residues of prior movement activity. Hatched (shaded) pictures and etchings cover variously colored and lighted planes, and thus belong to the visual arts proper. Sketches of figures and landscapes actually trace the path of the eye as it moves over the objects.

In linear drawing the flow of the movement is of the essence. In hatched drawing it is the plane which is covered. Thus, a linear pattern that is covered—or, worse, *filled in*—with hatched strokes, creates a mongrel beast, which mixes up the purpose of the two types of drawing as well as the spatial dimensions. When illustrating a landscape, be it imaginary or realistic, *holes in space* should not appear—the whole sheet of paper needs to be covered. When tracking a movement in space in linear form, we follow the motions and actually put down on paper the idea behind the movement. In this case a clean background, which is not *filled in* is appropriate, as it would detract from the purpose of such a linear drawing. Naturally we need to make an exception for technical drawings, such as object drawing or geometrical figures. Much has been written about pattern drawing, often called form drawing, or dynamic drawing; therefore we shall not enter into it more deeply here.

As writing is also a tracing of the movement, it becomes now apparent why Steiner set such value on the introduction of the letters through story, dramatic events and action.

Temperament Writing

Class teachers might have observed the following in their students: Around the ninth year, children's handwriting—reflecting a time of crisis—changes, often dramatically. Deterioration of form, sloppy writing, and diminutive letters may prevail for months, until, with a certain amount of prodding from the teacher, a more beautiful and harmonious style may be regained. The cause of the chaos is the re-orientation of the working of the formative forces. An incisive moment in the process of incarnation is reached. Before this time, children imitate the form principles created by adults and teachers. Now the imitated and learned forms fall apart, so that after the tenth-year crisis is over, children's own individualities work creatively into the very form principles of their handwriting. In short, children now search for their individual style of writing, while breaking down and discarding the imitated and previously acquired and learned style.

In their capacity of forming the bridge between individual and world, the temperaments may be employed successfully to aid children in this difficult transition. The very elements of writing may be shaped by earthy, airy, watery and fiery characteristics of form. Now we may, in the fourth grade, employ this differentiation of form characteristics in four clearly recognizable styles as a transitional form element towards the individualization of handwriting.

We let children write like craggy mountains

strong and hard city buildings, another.

74

Like the wavy ocean swells

wavy ocean swell

or like flirtatious wisps of cloud.

flirtatious whisps of cloud.—

We may employ this differentiation of style further in subjects such as grammar, for instance. Verbs could be written in a cholerically/fiery style, in red pencil of course; nouns melancholically/earthy, written in dark violet-blue; adjectives sanguinely/airy, written in bright yellow; and adverbs phlegmatically/watery, in green-blue color.

The above remarks must suffice to stimulate the reader to develop the work with the contractive and expansive principles right into the very form. With the above examples we remain still in the language of will. Needless to say, the reader has to elaborate from here into the language of feeling and rhythm and the language of imagery, in order to complete the whole process.

Sculpture

We begin movement activity in the archetypal form of the circle, representing the unstable equilibrium before creative action can take place. Similarly we may shape our material—beeswax or clay—in the archetypal sphere—the least differentiated and most universal shape.

In forming, by pressing into the center and pulling out toward the periphery, we sculpt in dynamic action and let the form become differentiated. The spherical forces of the head, the radial forces of the limbs, and the lemniscatory and curved forces, which form the equilibrium in transition and metamorphosis, dominate the very shaping of the human form.[36]

In contraction, when the spherical presses in towards the center, concave forms arise. In expansion, when the radial streams out towards the periphery, convex forms arise. In the equilibrium, when there is interplay between the forces from the outside and from the inside, curved and harmonious forms arise. When pressing in towards the center, we tend towards the earthy element; when bursting out towards the periphery, we tend towards the fiery element. Both air and water are in-between stages.

After the tenth year we might work with a group of children on a sequence of forms and shapes. In this way we may bring about a sequence of experiences which together stimulate the artistic process in our students. Although we have exaggerated here the two tendencies one-sidedly and thus have brought about a distortion, which is not beautiful, we would expect that at the hand of the one-sidedly ugly an aesthetic sense of discrimination would awaken in the students.

These shapes are but one indication of a sequence to stimulate the sculptural sensitivity in the fingertips. The starting point should be the center form. Then we would work towards one extreme, and finally towards the other. In this way we would school a student's sensitivity to concave and convex, expansive and contractive forms.

But what have the temperaments to do with all this, the reader might ask. The temperaments could be seen as the agents that help bring the process of creation into flow.

Temperaments in the Dynamics of the Artistic-Creative Process

The temperament activity in the artistic process is most closely related to the dynamics of the creative flow, to the correlation, transformation and metamorphosis of one stage of the process into the next. We bring to bear, as it were, each characteristic temperament/element essence in sequence upon the medium. As the process itself becomes dynamically alive, the various form elements of an art may converse with each other in their imponderable language.

We have the greatest clarity of characterization of the fourfold dynamics of a process in the musical arts. Indeed, I am convinced that only an imbuing with musicality will enable the teacher to infuse life into the artistic process. Thus I shall have to make use of musical concepts here in order to describe the dynamics of the artistic process.

1. Theme
2. Variations on the Theme
3. Conflict—Polarization and Dissonance
4. Balancing/Harmonizing
5. Resolution/Finale

There is a dramatic sequence in the parts of a symphony, for instance, which indicates the dynamic flow of artistic creation. For we have, first of all—considering sculpture—the basic substance: the lump of clay or the piece of stone. Then we have to bring some kind of force to bear on it, change it and transform it. As we work towards some kind of climax, the tension mounts. At last we find the harmonious resolution: A new form has arisen.

1. Substance at rest: that which is given.
2. Directed tension: application of energy.
3. Playful activity: pendulum swing between polar opposites.
4. Balancing the details, smoothing over, correlating details with the whole.
5. A dynamic equilibrium: a new form has arisen.

When working with these stages of a process, we work with time. The exact point at which the *leverage of the temperament* is necessary in order to bring the process into flux, to transform the static into the dynamic, is at the beginning of stage two—with our very first impression of our fingers upon the clay. With our fingers we can work in an earthy, watery, airy, and in a fiery manner.

Clay makes it easier to employ an earthy or a watery manner of treatment. Beeswax makes it possible to also work in an airy or a fiery manner. Wood again has its very own characteristics and invites a great deal of naturally watery, flowing forms. Stone and metal follow earthy and watery forms respectively.

As we reflect upon the two polarities active in individual and cosmos, we may describe once more the artistic process thus:

Step One: There is a static and fixed object, medium, or substance. It may have a definite shape or may be amorphous.

Step Two: This static material needs to be brought into motion. In order to enthuse her students, a great effort needs to be exerted upon them by the teacher. She has to inspire and challenge them with thought, story, question, description, and so forth, so that through the stirring of the imagination a fiery spark may kindle action and the creative process be enjoined.

Step Three: Now we push and pull and shape the clay in all six directions of space. Constantly polarizing/ balancing/ intensifying/playing as the music of the process unfolds.

Step Four: We begin to have an inkling of the final outcome. Amid often-traumatic birth pangs, the balancing and harmonizing take place.

Step Five: A new wholeness of form has come into being.

Of course this whole process assumes that free creation, out of the interplay between artist and substance, will take place, and that the artist is not constrained by a premeditated idea of what the outcome should be.

The first step—the stasis before creative action begins—is fundamentally of an earthy-contractive-melancholic nature. We have something that is tangible and material as a seed point, be it a piece of clay, wax, wood or stone.

The second step—in high contrast—is the point at which the greatest effort needs to be made, at which the greatest energy needs to expended. It is the choleric activity, the aggressiveness that attacks this passive material and aims to change it in every way. A choleric's ability to envision the future arouses inner fire, so that the transmuting process can begin. The teacher will find that a fiery mood will help release dynamic potentialities which slumber in the souls of children, so that they can indeed begin to work on the material. She needs to stimulate the fiery enthusiasm in each child.

Then, in the third step, the joys of playfulness abound as one tests the polarities, tastes one or the other pose and form, and gives full range to the *Spieltrieb*, the instinct and drive to play. Now all avenues are open, are tried out, all possibilities are considered, everything is attempted in the course of the airily sanguine third stage.

In the fourth step we balance out and harmonize. This requires a mercurially fluid and phlegmatic rhythm to help us finish off and round out all corners, as it were, satisfying the senses and putting the final touches to the work of balancing detailed facets with our concept of the whole.

In the fifth step we assure that the finished result is a living image of the concept, which has worked its way through to tangible form. That which has lived in our soul as the thought of the new form has now received—through the application of all four temperament/element stages—its new being and body. The creator—that is myself—stands face to face with the creature—my work.

Melancholics tend to remain longer with the first step—that is where they are most comfortable. Cholerics tend to bring their ego force to bear so powerfully that they shatter the material and transmute it only too well in dramatic action. Sanguines tend to remain with the playfulness, therefore they have difficulties in finishing. Instead they delight in the polarization without being able to finally resolve their work. Phlegmatics like to avoid the middle stages and go from the first to the last in a straight line—rounding off the given instead of effecting any actual transformation. A balanced person will go through all five stages, employing their dynamics in the act of creation. Thus any one temperament prefers its respective stage of the creative process.

The pathway of the creative process may thus lead from a melancholic beginning over a choleric transformation, sanguine playful experimentation and phlegmatic harmonization, to the new balanced whole. A given whole is pulled apart cholerically, mixed up sanguinely, fitted together again phlegmatically. For this reason all artistic-creative activity will help balance out one-sided temperament tendencies.

In as far as we aim at working with the universally human in all individuals, the activity of resolution and intensification, by overcoming polarization, represents the working of the Christ principle in relation to the polarized cosmic powers of Lucifer and Ahriman. Let us not forget that in order to be able to balance and resolve any manifestation of polarization, we ought to have the courage to let the opposing powers manifest and show themselves, in the first place. Thus: Let us not shrink from forming ahrimanic-demonic and luciferic-voluptuous shapes, but let us then resolve them, by leading them over into a balanced and harmonious form. Despite the danger of sounding pompous, I feel that it is essential to bring the Christ principle of balance to bear even upon the most modest artistic process. Steiner points to modern humanity's need to develop the feeling that an individual should become a seeker for the balancing position between the polarities.

Chapter Five

Color and the Visual Arts

There is a world of spirit, the world through which we pass between going to sleep and waking up. It is this world, which we bring with us out of sleep, which really inspires us when we paint, so that we are able at all to depict on canvas or wall the spiritual world which binds us in space. For this reason we must take great care to allow color to govern our painting, and not line. In painting, the line is a lie; the line is always part of the memory of life before birth. If we are to paint with a consciousness that extends across into the world of spirit, we must paint what comes out of the color. And we know that color is experienced in the astral world.[37]

— Rudolf Steiner

In the art of painting we work with fluid pigment. In drawing of any kind the resulting form is what is essential. But the form is already the result of prior movement or emotion. We need to recognize that the weaving of color comes before the fixedness of form.

There are, of course, many other visual arts techniques aside from painting. In each of them the interplay of light and dark creates life, whereas the fixed form arises through the rigidity of line. The fluid medium of the painter's pigment enhances the possibility of an interaction between light and dark. For this reason we shall concern ourselves principally with painting in this chapter, and make only a few comments on some of the drawing techniques.

In sculpture as well as in the pre-sculptural movement arts, as we have outlined above in Chapter 4, a person's formative forces are enticed to work into the forces of the physical body. In painting the astral principles of light and darkness, the star forces of consciousness, of sympathy and antipathy, are active within the flow of time, of rhythm, of process. Form here is born of the interaction of light and darkness, of color, of the joys and sufferings of the light, as Goethe put it.

If we do the same in connection with the astral body, as it were pushing what is in us of an astral nature a step lower down into the etheric body, we are pushing down what lives inwardly in man. Now nothing arises that could truly have a spatial nature, for the astral body, when it moves down into the etheric body, is not entering a spatial element: the etheric body is rhythmic and harmonious, not spatial. Therefore what arises can only be a picture, indeed a real picture, in fact the art of painting.[38]

Painting is the temperament art par excellence, for the home of painting is within the very same realm of the inner human being where the temperaments also work and weave—in the interplay between the astral/consciousness/movement and etheric/life/formative nexus of human forces.

The Interaction of Light and Darkness in Relation to the Temperaments

In considering the disposition for contraction and expansion as a fundamental principle of the etheric forces, we may assign the colors red and yellow to the expansive side of the spectrum and blue and violet to the contractive side. Green holds a middle position. It is elucidating here to refer to the following three states of human incarnation according to Sankhya philosophy as described by Rudolf Steiner.

It is sattwa, for example, when the spiritual predominates over the natural. It would be correct to say that red and reddish-yellow represent the sattwa condition of light. Aristotle no longer used this terminology, but he still retained the principle of the old Sankhya philosophy where green represents the rajas condition as regards light and darkness and blue and violet, in which darkness predominates, represent the tamas condition.[39]

The rajas condition is the condition of balance between the spiritual and the natural within a person, and the tamas condition is the predominance of the natural over the spiritual. The color spectrum thus shows three possible forms of relationship between a person's spiritual and natural being. With this we have one key for the translating of soul elements into physical manifestation. Above all we have here a key for the deliberate use of artistic elements in a meaningful as opposed to an haphazard manner. Yet we need to make further steps towards an understanding of the nature of color before concerning ourselves with its application in the art of painting. In his lectures on color, Rudolf Steiner presents a basic seven foldness in the realm of color: The three luster colors—yellow, blue, red; and the four image colors—white, green, peach and black.

As a young man, Steiner edited Goethe's scientific works, making a particular study of and writing a detailed introduction to his *Theory of Color*. While acknowledging Goethe's incisive importance in developing a phenomenological approach to science, Steiner felt the need to take further steps in this direction. He closed his lectures on color with the following words:

> *In Goetheanism we find a way of knowledge, which embraces the realm of soul and spirit but which needs to be developed further. Goethe, for example, was not able to reach the distinction between image and lustre colors. We must follow Goethe's approach in a living way in our thinking so that we can continually go further. This can only be done through spiritual science.*[40]

Luster colors:

Yellow	Red	Blue

Image colors:

White	Peach	Green	Black

Why does Rudolf Steiner make this distinction between luster and image colors? The primary colors—yellow, red, blue—are astral colors: The soul principle preponderates. White, peach, green and black are image colors—the etheric-form principle preponderates.

In painting we may either paint more strongly from the luciferic/astral side, or more from the ahrimanic/etheric side of the color range. Depending on the theme and subject matter, we may choose to use the group of colors more related to one or the other side. Steiner also gives some complex indications of how image and luster colors should be used when painting nature—mineral, plant, animal and man.

The artist knows that when he handles yellow, blue and red, he must induce in his picture something that expresses an inwardly dynamic quality which itself gives character. If he is working with peach blossom and green on black and white then he knows that an image quality is already present in the color. Such a science of color is so inwardly living that it can pass immediately from the soul's experience into art. [41]

It follows that in a painting with a representational theme the image colors by their very nature support the formative contents. If, however, mood and emotion should be important, then the luster colors need to be used. It is good to remind ourselves here that few twentieth century painters use pure luster colors. The mixing of black and white with all pigments has become fashionable and is typical of our time. This results in luster colors being painted as if they were image colors. One could say then that the soul element is eliminated to a large extent.

Further, one may consider that it is traditional in Waldorf schools to use the luster colors predominantly for young children and on into the early grades, whereas the image colors are introduced around third grade. This tradition reflects the viewpoint that young children live more strongly in the world of emotions and empathy and grow into precisely observing the external forms of objects at a later age.

The being of color has its soul in the luster colors and its body in the image colors. To paint predominantly in image colors means to pay more heed to the body than to the soul.

The interaction of light and darkness comes to its most hardened and defined expression in the juxtaposition of black and white; it comes to soul-filled expression in the juxtaposition between blue and yellow. Red mediates and intensifies both the soul experience of the contrasting interaction of light and dark. Rudolf Steiner called green, as red's complementary color, the dead image of the living. It mediates also, but outwardly. Both colors hold a mediating position within the contractive and expansive, the ahrimanic and luciferic, the etheric and astral forces.

There is a similarity between the inner dynamic inherent in the sevenfold range of colors and the threefoldness with the fourfoldness, which express the seasons of the year. [42] A dynamic threefoldness is, as it were, at the back of the more outwardly perceptible fourfoldness of the four seasons of the year. We understand the cyclical change of the seasons best by realizing that a season of differentiation—in winter—passes over into a season of unification in summer. Spring and autumn are the transitional seasons linking the two. Similarly we may develop a feeling for the dynamics of color by understanding blue as the color leading to more differentiated forms and thus as it were endowing us with a winter feeling; yellow leading us towards unification, engendering a summer feeling; and red—which can stand to be painted as a solid surface in contrast to the other two colors—in a position of equilibrium.

The image of complete differentiation—or winter—would be black; the image of summer—total unification—would be white; thus going from winter to summer would be peach blossom—this is marked by Easter; the going from summer to winter would be green—this is marked by the Michaelmas festival. Steiner makes the following remarks in his notebooks about peach and green:

> Peach blossom: where the soul holds sway in life and everything dead is neutralized. . . .
> In green: death has spread itself out—life is dried up.[43]

It is not without significance that in paintings of Michael and the dragon, the dragon is usually painted green. The dragon forces are an expression of the nature forces, which tend toward decline and into outer death at Michaelmas. Equally, the peach-magenta color is the very image of the promise of life in spring, of the promise of the resurrection of the life forces in nature at Easter.

We may now understand that painting is not a *filling in* of an image designed by the mind, but a living process in which we let the colors speak to each other. These last remarks hint at the possibility to develop a feeling for a deeper meaning behind the individual colors.

Here we need to remember Steiner's statement that the true aesthetic experience comes about through the enlivening of the sensory processes and the ensoulment of the life processes. One painter, drawing on her experience, said:

> One's sense of smell comes into play—and Rudolf Steiner describes how one smells the intervals. This is a process belonging mainly to the air, but one can sense the fragrance of the color intervals. The intervals are in the air that we smell.

One says: he smells of holiness; or something smells fishy; or it stinks. It is our air-body that smells intervals of color. One can in time become conscious of this and of tasting the colors, especially with plant colors more than with other colors. . . . The interval between color and color—whatever it is, it represents the penetration of the spiritual. The interval allows the penetration of the spiritual into the soul element.[44]

Painting as a Living Process

Painting becomes an enlivening activity if we follow the principle of enacting a process rather than dispensing information in visual form in our pedagogical endeavors. Such a dynamic process is in itself a means of balancing aimless and undisciplined self-expression, that is, an experiment of playing with color, with the rigid filling in of a pre-determined form. The former, playful self-expression, may deteriorate into senseless playfulness; the latter, may harden into following a premeditated illustration. Neither polarity is easily transformed into a true work of art.

As we pointed out in the previous chapter, a process has an inner musical dynamic, not unlike a discourse between individuals. Individuals participating in a conversation determine the direction the conversation will take through their own character. In this way the inner dynamic unfolds. Different color individualities, if I may call them such, will interact according to their inherent qualities and inclinations, revealing their own character. If I start on a white sheet of paper by painting a blue spot, I have first of all the lively relationship of blue and white: blue will tend—if we live ourselves feelingly into its essence—to surround the white and, apparently, swallow it up. It will tend to bore a hole into the paper and remove what it encloses into the distance. If we add another color—say, yellow—these two will interact, unfolding a story in the fluid medium of painting. If the colors are in liquid form, then this interaction will become all the more dynamic. For pedagogical considerations, it is important to point out that Steiner makes specific recommendations to let children paint out of the pure color experience of the luster colors in the first years of the elementary school. The representational-conceptual element, the element demanding more work with the image colors, should be introduced later, around the ninth year of age.

Several years after the founding of the first Waldorf school, Steiner speaks of the parasitic nature of our present-day civilization. Even spiritual impulses cannot be taken up easily by human beings, as there is a tendency for them to turn into poison if not understood (*Man as Symphony of the Creative Word,* op. cit., Lecture of November 11, 1923). He continues there:

> *During his years of education a great deal is brought to the child of this parasitic nature. We must, therefore, develop an art of education, which works creatively from his soul. We must let the child bring color into form; and the color-forms, which have arisen out of joy, out of enthusiasm, out of sadness, out of every possible feeling, these he can paint on to the paper. When a child puts on to the paper what arises out of his soul, this develops his humanity. This produces nothing parasitic. This is something, which grows out of man like his fingers or his nose! —Whereas, when the child has forced on him the conventional forms of the letters, which are the results of a high degree of civilization, this does engender what is parasitic. Immediately the art of education lies close to the human heart, the human soul, the spiritual approaches man without becoming poison. First you have the diagnosis, which finds that our age is infested with carcinomas, and then you have the therapy—yes, it is Waldorf school education.*

In a conference with the teachers of the Waldorf School in Stuttgart—November 15, 1920—Steiner answered a teacher's question about painting in the following way:

> *You will get your forms, if you allow their [the children's] fantasy to work. You must let these forms grow out of the colors. You can talk to the children directly in a color language. Just think how stimulating it would be to enable them to understand you when you say: Here is this coquettish mauve, and on his neck a cheeky little red fellow is sitting. In the background there is a meek and humble blue. If colors become as concrete as objects, they will help to*

develop the soul. Let colors activate the soul. Everything which arises out of color itself can be applied in fifty differ- ent ways. You must let the children live in the experience of color by saying, for instance, 'Here the red is peeping through the blue,' and then really get the children to bring this about on paper. You should try to bring a great deal of life into this. By stimulating them in this way, you free them from a kind of lumpishness, sluggishness. Speaking generally, it is important for our time that living in the experience of color is cultivated and deepened. This in turn will stimulate the musical element.[45]

The above indications demand essentially that we develop a class-room technique which will allow us to let children experience this dy-namic interaction of colors as a process, which may lead to the forming of shapes out of the color. Let us be clear, though, that what this means is, that when forms arise from color, astral forces work into the etheric forces. Following are two scenarios which describe possible approaches to enact such color conversations.

Two Examples
Scenario One
This is a possible scenario suitable for younger children. The paint-ing lesson is prepared. All have liquid paints, two water jars (one in which to wash brushes, another with *clean* water to allow for optional toning down of strong color). The paper is on the board. Brushes and sponges (not for wiping off paint from the paper, but for the drying of the brushes) are at the ready. The teacher also has her or his materials ready. The teacher's demonstration paper is either on the blackboard or on a separate table around which all the children are gathered.

Teacher: "Once upon a time there was a very, very sad blue. Look! —It sits here all by itself. How would you sit if you were very sad?" Some children reply, there is some discussion, then the teacher paints a blue sad shape on the paper. She points out that this would be her own sad shape, and that each child would also have to find her or his very own blue sad shape. With words such as the above we encourage children to enter into the color with empathy and feeling, and find the form which arises natu-rally out of this feeling—in this case definitely a melancholic shape in the contractive color blue.

After completing the blue form we might continue, "And now—suddenly—a very impudent yellow jumps right into the paper. See!—It looks at the sad blue and decides to tease it—here, and here, and here. It really is not malicious, only playful and intends cheering up the sad blue. At first the blue misunderstands the yellow—it is frightened, but soon it begins to answer, and before long the yellow and the blue speak with each other. Look what happens then." (We allow a full green to arise—of course we must have the right shades of blue and yellow: Prussian blue and lemon yellow mix well, as do cobalt blue and cadmium yellow.) We let the children paint the sanguine yellow, making sure that yellow does not get too fixed and solid. The nature of yellow really demands a very sanguine treatment.

You will see that a yellow surface with definite boundaries is a repulsive thing; it is quite unbearable to artistic feeling. The soul cannot bear a yellow surface which is limited. We must make yellow paler at the edges, then paler still; in short the yellow must be full in the center, shining out into a still paler yellow. If we are to experience its inner nature we cannot imagine yellow in any other way. YELLOW MUST SHINE OUTWARDS.[46]

In the course of the above painting event, children may experience a process of dynamic interaction between the inherently sanguine nature of the yellow and the inherently melancholic nature of the blue. Of course, even our very brush stroke will go along with the inherent tendency of each color. We will apply the blue in smooth and gentle strokes and follow the shape we have in mind lovingly. The yellow will be put on in shorter strokes, we could call them dancing strokes, as they flash out from the center, out from the brilliant spot of yellow, to brighten in flashes the rest of the paper and interact with the blue. Thus our very hand movements will carry meaning right into the brush and onto the paper. Our loving awareness will thus permeate from heart to hand.

In young children or in children not familiar with a Waldorf approach, this type of scenario, if repeated over a period of time, helps to develop a feeling for the living soul mood carried by the primary colors and later by the secondary colors. With older children this approach, which relies so strongly on the capacity for imitation in the younger child, would be too restrictive, and would thus prove to be counterproductive. We need to fire their imagination a different way.

Scenario Two

Again, we assume that the students have made all necessary preparations under the guidance of the teacher. (The teacher needs to decide on the colors, for only she or he can determine which color experiences are needed. Over a year one should build up and develop the color experiences systematically and not haphazardly.) This time the teacher will not paint in order for the students to observe or imitate her, but she might well paint for herself, once the class has started and all are absorbed in their tasks.

Teacher: "Remember what we discussed in main lesson yesterday? Who would like to tell us?"—"Yes, Hannibal's crossing of the Alps. Now imagine that you are standing on the North side of one of the Alpine passes, watching his army, elephants and all, make their way and winding gradually up and up, dangerously close to fearful chasms and steep slopes. They are retreating from you, vanishing between the ice and snow covered peaks. Now imagine something else! Imagine that you were on the South side of the Alps, in the fertile foothills, watching the army descend, wind down the steep paths, coming closer and closer to you. Tell me, which colors would you use for painting the first scene, and which colors would be more suitable for the second scene?"

Hopefully a lively discussion will follow. By guiding it carefully we may elicit from the children the answer that the first scene should be painted principally in blue/violet/white shades of color, whereas the second scene mostly in yellow/red and orange. "Now, you may choose on which side of the Alps you would like to be. Choose your colors accordingly! Remember, if you are on the South slopes, the oncoming armies threaten you! If you are on the North slopes, then you will feel relief as they disappear beyond the horizon."

And thus, arising from a discussion with the class, a feeling for color perspective may be engendered in a sixth grade. Note also that in the second scenario the participation of each child is necessary, and also stimulated, so that inner activity and involvement come about as the very painting proceeds. It is vital for teachers to realize that only by stimulating the inner picturing capacities will students become really creative in their artistic work. We cannot stimulate individual creativity by asking students to copy what we have done. We can, however, teach technique by asking for imitation of brushstroke, and so forth. These indications are for a Waldorf grade school teacher. We must realize that in the high school there are other demands and perspectives.

Obviously, this type of introduction will be successful only if the students have had experience in this color approach, as well as good skills in brushwork, and know altogether how to handle the materials. Thus the teaching of the appropriate technique is also essential. Some classes may be oriented toward the learning and practicing of technique, others to individual expression of what lives in the students' souls as an inner picture of the topic. A side remark: Painting, as any of the other arts, is not used to illustrate realistically an intellectual content, nor is it developed as *art for art's sake* in Waldorf education, but serves as a medium for learning. Through all the arts the student's whole being is united with the contents of the lesson—in this case Roman history—not only his intellect. Thus heart and head and hand are brought into active relationship with each other in each student, as the living symphony of contractive and expansive colors comes to life in the painting of each child. Temperament characteristics, qualities and peculiarities are integral parts of this whole learning experience—thus the work of each child will reveal directly the temperamental inclinations through the choice of color, tone and shape in image form. Those teachers who have developed a feeling for the temperaments will thus be able to interpret the work of each student according to temperament modulations.

Characteristic Dynamics of Painting

As remarked above, painting is the temperament art par excellence—for method and content, essence and form combine here to reveal the elemental fourfoldness in its contractive-expansive nature. The very strokes of the brush should emulate the temperament of the color one paints—dancing strokes for yellow, smooth longer ones for blue, and so forth. Van Gogh's brushstrokes show clearly a choleric forcefulness; Turner's an airy light-filled sanguinity, which has tinges of the watery phlegmatic in its smoothness; with Seurat and Sisley, for instance, sanguinity to the extreme; in Chagall the melancholic tinged with the choleric. I am suggesting that the gestalt formation of the brush stroke reveals the basic temperament tendency of the painter. It is interesting to note that most painters treat all colors with the same brush stroke. Does this mean that only the really great painters are able to infuse their temperament right into the brushstroke?

In the first scenario the imitative approach is indicated: Color as the guise of a typical temperament creates a story on paper or canvas, which we develop step by step together with the students.

In scenario two we fire the child's imagination. He or she then chooses to identify with one or the other suggestion, with one or the other side—contractive or expansive—of the temperament spectrum. I have often found it vital to give children of ten years or older a choice of two, or even three, approaches to one topic. The student identifies then with the teacher's vivid verbal description and is thus able to call up an inner feeling and picture before painting what is inwardly perceived. If we would make older children imitate, we would hamper, not further, their creative work. It is important to notice the developmental state at which we can proceed to stimulate the child's fantasy by way of this inner participation in what we present.

Color exercises begin in the early years, at first with the primary colors, then the secondary colors. These color dialogues prepare the child's ability to proceed to the representational/image character of painting from the ninth year on. It goes without saying that there is no need to refrain rigidly from using the second approach once in a while even with younger children. From time to time students need to be challenged to reach their limits. One of the greatest difficulties in the medium of wet-on-wet watercolor painting is to learn the transitions from one color to the adjoining one—careful brushwork, as well as control of liquidity, is essential and needs to be practiced from the early grades onward.

But by and large we work first with the soul qualities of color, and then in later years we add the image qualities. This approach accompanies the incarnation process harmoniously. The development of thinking also corresponds to this development, from the soul-filled to the more image-filled, in the course of the elementary school years.

It is necessary to note here how all three temperament languages are employed in painting: The color exercises deal with luster colors and convey meaning as form/gestalt/gesture arises from color; the dynamics of rhythmic motion comes to expression in the brush stroke; we feel with the color as the story of the interaction develops, colors leaping forward or retreating out of the white paper; and gradually the image coalesces. The sequence of having an inner picture before we begin, then the activity of putting color to paper, then adjusting, changing, harmonizing, allowing colors to interact, and finally fine-tuning to express the meaning clearly—all are steps already discussed as the key picture of the learning process in Chapter 2.

The flowing mercurial medium of the liquid paints is essential for a pedagogical approach to painting. Steiner comments:

> *We should try to paint increasingly from pots of liquid paint with color that is liquid and has a flowing, shining quality. Generally speaking, the introduction of the palette has brought an inartistic element into painting. The palette has brought a materialistic form of painting, a failure to understand the true nature of color—for color is never really absorbed by any material body but lives within it and emanates from it. Therefore, when I put my colors on to a surface I must make them shine inwardly.*[47]

Moreover, in the intensification or dilution we have yet another aspect of the contractive-expansive polarity. The fluid element is the *body* of color, the airy element is the *soul* of color, and this relationship is accurately reflected in the smallest detail of the painting process. This points us to the interaction between etheric forces—the formative life forces—and astral forces—the emotional-movement-consciousness forces (see Chapter 9). The airy element dissolves the color into light and air; the watery element makes the color strong, rich, and tangible. An earthy element may creep in which causes the pigment to dry up and to solidify.

As mentioned above, because of this intimate relation of painting and temperament, we may observe a particular tendency in the mode in which a person creates forms, uses colors, handles the brush and applies liquid. In short, we may read a person's temperament very accurately from the way he or she paints.

Typical Temperament Painting

If left to themselves, melancholics will tend to paint in the dark colors—blue, violet, brown and black. Their paper will likely become dry very quickly and their forms will be small, sharp, and with defined edges.

Their brush strokes will probably be unrhythmical, uneven and show diffidence. Cholerics will paint generously with bright, deep colors, rich reds and oranges, wide forceful brush strokes, large, often well-defined and aggressive forms. Sanguines will paint often in colors that appear faded and light. They tend to use yellow, green, orange, and are often cheerfully patchy. The composition as a whole will be pleasing to the eye, but the details will tend to look a little unfinished. Phlegmatics will tend to choose the cool colors, the blues, greens and violets. Forms will be softer and bulkier than in the typical melancholic painting. Their strokes will be large, even overflowing the page. Some phlegmatics can fill up a piece of paper with regular undifferentiated strokes or with undifferentiated blobs of color. Moreover, the liquidity will be strong, so that colors will run into each other easily, and the definition of form will tend to become diluted.

As the teacher walks from student to student and watches, helps and suggests, she or he will, of course, be able to modify and encourage many extremes into a harmonious composition. One reason for the teacher to "interfere" with the work of students is to present examples of brushstroke, detail work, loving attention to the process, as well as to suggest details regarding color tone and intensity, and so on. Painting thus becomes an art most centrally related to working with the temperaments—that is, leading the fundamental tendency into a more balanced expression, if necessary. Let it be noted, that we do not *correct* the temperament, but it is in the social interest that each individual be able to modify any extreme tendencies. Let it be noted again, that it is very rare for one child to exhibit one temperament modulation to the extreme. In most individuals all four tendencies are present, but one or the other (even two) may predominate.

This chapter is about the visual arts. So far we have spoken only about painting, and not about any other visual technique. The three-dimensionality of space in a picture needs to arise through the color interaction in the work of the younger children. But with students over twelve years of age, due to their particular developmental stage, other approaches may be used to expand their experience with the expansive-contractive polarity. For this reason several drawing techniques have been suggested by Steiner. Bearing in mind that we will now deal with representational drawing, and not the pattern drawing arising from movement, we shall describe these various techniques and their purposes briefly.

Drawing and the Temperaments

It is important to realize that the medium of drawing with crayons or pencils allows the principles of form to come to the foreground far more strongly than with the fluidity of paints. Thus there is no way that the living element of color can be experienced quite so fully in drawing as in painting.

Geometrical patterns belong to the family of pattern drawings that arise from motion. They are really a form of technical drawing, directly related to mathematics, though the patterns created through the intricate web of number relationships as expressed in geometry can be profoundly stimulating and revealing to the growing mind and enthuse students for mathematics.

Steiner indicates that it is important for children around the tenth year to learn to draw objects by direct observation. At this age the child has, as described more fully in Chapter 8, come to him- or herself. The child now looks out into the world from a different viewpoint than before and is able to acquire greater self-confidence and to observe more accurately and in greater detail the world through the vehicle of the senses. The sense of motion is involved when we trace the forms of the objects around us with our eyes.

It is important that the child's awakening faculties should be used. An accurate observation of the objects situated in the space around us obliges us to develop a sensitivity for relative position, degree of shadow, and a feeling for texture. These are all qualities only marginally related to the area of experience described in painting. They are qualities related more to the physical properties of the objects around us, and thus, in a sense, we could just as easily use photography. Object drawing is important for children not because it employs the soul forces, but because the eye is trained to take note of the physical phenomena accurately and in loving detail.

There is, however, one drawing technique which engenders a certain flow, and thus provides a possibility of lively interweaving of light and dark in the realm of color. This technique, often called *shading* in Waldorf schools, employs a hatching stroke (in one particular direction, usually from the right top of the paper to the left bottom corner, because this is the natural direction for right handed individuals). By learning to cover paper fairly rapidly with short hatching strokes, an interaction of colors may be achieved which allows a certain elemental interweaving of light and dark to take place, so that the essence of color shines through the strokes. Forms also arise out of the movement and the color.

The very same hatching stroke may also be used in the upper grades of the elementary school and in the high school for work with charcoal. This is an important aspect of the work in the visual arts, for when working with black on white the contrast of the contrac-  tive-expansive forces is polarized further, and thus made more tangible. This medium is particularly appropriate for the pre-puberty years of the student; we place darkness into the light deliberately. In learning to deal with black and white, darkness and light, and the innumerable gradations and values arising in the intermediate stages, adolescents are given help to prepare them to deal with the black and white, the darkness and the light, within their own souls, within the thoughts, emotions and instincts which will surely assail them in the course of the next few years.

Altogether, the hatching stroke, whether used with color or with black, provides a harmonious interplay of all three soul forces with the human self. For this reason the tenth year is a good time to insist on the correct applica-  tion of this technique. Another aspect of the hatching stroke is that it represents a polarity to precisely linear object drawing. In object drawing, we focus with great intensity on an object. When using the hatching stroke, our eyes do not focus, per se, with intensity on an external object, but we may use peripheral vision, where our inner picture may meld with the fluidity of color or light and dark, as the case may be.

The feeling element is addressed by the interweaving of the strokes. The intentionality of the soul, the capacity for directed action, is engaged by the effort and challenge to keep the strokes in the same direction, to keep them even, parallel and separate from each other. The forms that arise, or that one intends putting onto paper, address the cognitive and reflective element.

And what of the ego, the individual self? The forces of the self are engaged in keeping the balance between all three, so that a picture may arise. The self shows itself, as it were, in the interstices, in the intervals. The self works through the intangible, through the relatedness of all three elements; but in that very intangibility it makes itself felt, for its absence as the main organizing factor would be noted immediately.

Here, too, the different temperaments reveal themselves through their language of form, color, and intensity. Cholerics will tend to press down too hard on the paper and make large strokes, bold colors and shapes will arise. Melancholics will tend to make small strokes, use dark colors, work slowly and have difficulties in covering the whole paper evenly. Sanguines will work haphazardly. Phlegmatics will work beautifully but have difficulties in letting forms actually consolidate. Consequently, this is a technique eminently suitable for the healthy balancing of extreme temperament tendencies.

Also here, as with painting, all three temperament languages come into play: The language of gesture and movement expresses itself in the quality of the very hatching stroke; the language of rhythm in the flow and repetitiveness of the strokes and of their interweaving; the language of image crystallizes into form—either with color or in the starkness of the black on white. Thus all three are addressed.

The strokes may be fiery, earthy, watery or airy; the rhythmicality may show the same fourfold differentiation; the images themselves may be born out of the fiery, the airy, the watery or the earthy element. So we learn to distinguish the typical temperament modes in all three languages in the visual arts media.

The Influence of the Polarizing Powers on Painting

Steiner mentions that the art of painting is particularly exposed to the influences of the two cosmic powers. In spite of occupying a middle position amongst the arts, painting is a fertile field of temptation to leave balance and harmony and err into one or the other extreme.

Lucifer tempts the painter to indulge in effusive haziness, a mystic glow of reds and yellows, or voluptuous and insinuating forms. Color is apparently more important than form. The sensuous beauty of Gauguin's paintings, in all their magnificence, is surely inspired by Lucifer. Even the musicality, which Gauguin evokes in his color intervals (he methodically developed a concordance of music and color), points to the Luciferic-expansive influence.

Turner, also, though in a more refined manner, gives himself up to the ethereally airy: He raises up the landscape to glowing beauty. Without Lucifer there would be no beauty.

Ahrimanic influences harden and solidify form and darken color into strident and dark tones. Salvador Dali—a surrealist—would press all into one form principle. Note also his predilection for green, grey and black! Also, the distortion, fragmentation and dissection of the human form, which glare from many of his paintings, show the influence of the contractive principle. *Nay,* we could cry out, *he presses through the form principle into its dissolution—the caricature.* This influence is a splintering influence. Other natural forms are also splintered in Dali's paintings, not only the human form. Surely also the recent tendency to produce gigantic *objects* and present them as art must be laid at the door of the ahrimanic influence to tip the scales in favor of the material at the cost of the spiritual.

The Pre-Raphaelites, on the other hand—altogether all the cloying illustrators of sentimentally mystic and fantastic persuasions—are under Lucifer's sway. It is not easy today to deal with an aberration, that would present the fantastic and illusionary as something of a truly spiritual origin. This influence is much more difficult to refute as it is more insidious.

In our century we have seen the coming of the photographic piecemeal and the phantasmagoric illusionary as the Scylla and Charybdis of the painterly voyage: Temptation in this modern odyssey beckons from both sides. Like Odysseus, who had to listen with his inner ear, we could say that the painter today needs to see with the inner eye, so that he or she learns to extend the naturally given form principles arising from color. The starting point must be the pure phenomena of nature and her or his aim the loving continuation of the work of nature. Then also in this art may we permeate artistic striving with the Christ principle of harmonizing the extremes in an ever-present battle for the finding of balance.

Chapter Six

Music and the Twofold Ego Experience

Music takes up no space but is solely present in time. In the same way, what matters with regard to the human etheric body in reality (not in the imaginative picture we draw) is mobility, movement, formative activity in rhythmic or musical sequence, in fact the quality of time. Of course, this is a difficult thing for the human mind to conceive, accustomed as it is to relating everything to space; but in order to gain a clear concept of the etheric body we must try much harder to allow musical ideas rather than spatial ideas to come to our aid.[48]

— Rudolf Steiner

Have you ever listened to Indian or African music? Have you allowed it to vibrate in your body, as it streams into your very muscles and beats a path from the earth upwards in sensuous insistence? Have you contrasted it with the music of Bach, for instance, whose cerebral harmonies make transparent the crystalline spheres of the cosmos? Then you will have felt in you the deep chasm between the Dionysian and the Apollonian elements in music.

Earth-born is the one—beating upwards through our body on the waves of blood and setting our feet in dancing motion as they catch the rhythm. Cosmos-born is the other—of the cosmic widths and majestic rhythms of the planetary orbs resounding in subtle harmonies. Their origins are apparently disparate, yet each type of music is due to the organizing work of our essential self within our astral bodies, that is, our configuration of consciousness and mind.

We need to refer here to the twofold ego, the twofold essence of our spirit, our self. The ego sends its activity into our soul forces from two directions, as it were, from the past through our head and the nervous/sensory system, and from the future through our body and its blood and muscles.

Apollo's lyre constitutes the human nervous system upon which he—Apollo, representative of the upper ego—plays his divine music. Rudolf Steiner makes use of this image repeatedly when characterizing the nervous system. On the other hand, our muscles in conjunction with the sense of movement constitute the instrument of Dionysus, as he stirs our limbs from below. Steiner makes this point, with some others of equally eminent importance to teachers, in his lectures on *Balance in Teaching* (Mercury Press, Spring Valley, 1982, GA 302a, Lecture of September 21, 1920):

> *That which in the ear comprises the sense organization is inwardly linked in a very delicate way with all those nerves known to present-day physiology as 'motor nerves,' but which in reality are identical with the sensory nerves; so that everything we experience as resonant sound is perceived through the nerve-strands embedded in our limb organization. Everything musical, if it is to be perceived in the right way, must first penetrate deep into our whole organization—and for this the nerves of the ear are appropriately organized— and must affect that region of the nerves otherwise reached only by the will. For those regions in the human organism that in the case of pictorial experiences make memory possible are the very ones that in the case of the musical, the audible element, give rise to perception.*

We may conclude that tremendous secrets of existence and of human incarnation are involved in the complex, delicate and vital interplay of the forces of the head with the rest of the body.

The Twofold Self and the Form of Musical Instruments

Let us take a further step in attempting to understand the working of the ego into human astrality in the realm of music. If we take the element of air as the one through which the astral forces work, we need to focus on the manner in which air is brought to vibrate in generating musical sound. We may see a parallel between string instruments and the human nervous system. In both, the agent of vibration

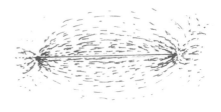

is on the inside of the body of air, which is set to vibrate. They are both stirred, as it were, by the inner ego forces, by Apollo.

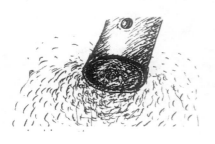

On the other hand, consider the flute, or any other instrument, which encloses the vibrating air body. (Let us distinguish clearly that in the string instruments the sound is amplified by the sound box, but not created by it.) Here the moving power is brought to bear from the outside onto the enclosed air. This is parallel to the outer ego as it moves our limbs from the outside.

Dionysus stirs our limbs from without. Looking at a human being as an instrument of music, we may distinguish high tones—that is, head tones—and low tones—that is, chest tones. Our larynx is like an inverted flute, our whole lung the sound box of a Dionysian instrument and our diaphragm a resonating drum skin. Later we shall mention more about the human body in relation to pitch. Let is suffice here to point out that the higher tones are *nerve* tones, the lower *blood* tones.

Although, superficially speaking, one describes the vibrations of the air as carrying a tone, on looking closer we find that really the fluid element is the basis of sound. It is the element which carries the working of the tone ether. Steiner also calls this ether the number or chemical ether, for it carries within it the element of relationship expressed as ratio or number. He speaks of the life of the cosmos, which is pure ether, of the orbiting of the planets in their spheres in ever changing mobile rhythms, which resist becoming perfect numerical ratios, for then the solar system would become a rigid mechanism. Thus Steiner describes the irrational element of number as being proof of cosmic life. The irregularities in the planetary orbits and stellar motions are proof of their very life: Countless cyclical repetitions occur, which are yet never exactly the same, and thus avoid a fate of rigid fixation. The historical age which attempted to fix these ratios, the modern age, made by implication mechanical clockwork out of the cosmos. This development was accompanied by the deadening of thinking.

The human ego element is the organizing principle which introduces these variations upon a theme. One also could describe the ego, the human innermost spiritual essence, as the carrier of the irrational.

One of the deepest secrets of the Greek Mysteries is, according to Steiner, that Apollo and Dionysus are one and the same. The same ego works from the past and from the future in an individual. It works into the astral body in both the Apollonian and the Dionysian modes such that a balance can be prepared which is capable of housing the Christ. In his profound lecture on *Blood and Nerves (Toward Imagination, Culture and the Individual,* Anthroposophic Press, Hudson, NY, 1990, GA 169, Lecture of June 13, 1916), Steiner describes the nerve substance in our body as being cosmically alive and dead only on earth, whereas the substance of our blood carries death forces within it and receives its life from the outside, from the cosmos. Real life is altogether not found on earth, only outside the earth, in the cosmos. The nerve substance, as it were, gives its life to the blood. Thus it receives death on its way to become earthly, but blood must become alive so that each human, in as far as he or she consists of earthly substance, may turn to the cosmos.

Christ brought the very life of our nerves from the cosmos onto the earth—that self-same life which mankind had to leave behind in the cosmos—so that now it could unite with the blood, which stems from the earth. Apollo—the sun god—resides in the upper regions. He moves his instruments from the outside, from the heavens as it were, and imparts them with life. Cosmic life stirs the dead form.

Dionysus is a child of the earth. Earthly life has to die. In volcanic upheaval, in outbursts of passion, which aim at death—and which, in mythology, often ended in death—he beats the drum of life; he stirs the chaotic unconscious will of the body.

Christ united these polarities so that in each human being the chasm between head and body, nerve and blood should be bridged. Steiner relates the Christ mystery directly to music. He characterizes the intervals, as they were perceived by humanity in the course of evolution. The interval of the third became discernable only in the Christian era.

> *Therefore what I described as an interval of the third can correspond either to the astral body or to the sentient soul: in the one case we have the major third and in the other the minor third.* [49]

In the experience of the interval of the third we have the bridge between the outer and the inner worlds. Musical experience itself may furnish us with an approach towards an understanding of the essence of Christ, as Steiner indicates here:

> *The coming of the figure of Christ, the spiritually-living figure, which I referred to as the culminating point in human evolution, has been magnificently portrayed in Renaissance and pre-Renaissance painting, but in future will have to be expressed through music.*[50]

Steiner then describes in detail the necessary sequence of intervals to evoke this musical experience, ending thus:

> *We find here a means of passing in an intensely minor mood from the dissonances of the seventh, from the near consonance of these diminishing dissonances to the sphere of the fifth in a minor mood, and from that point blend the sphere of the fifth with that of the minor third, then we shall have evoked in this way the musical experience of the Incarnation, and what is more, of the Incarnation of the Christ.*[51]

We have approached the realm of music in such sweeping strokes, with such wide implications, because music has a great bearing upon the future of humanity as well as each individual. It is linked intimately with our inner and eternal being. It is connected with our life of volition, and thus musical experience and activity during childhood is essential for the engendering of a sound foundation of volitional capacities for adult life. Moreover, the concern with the musical essence of an individual and of the cosmos in itself is helpful to the teacher in coming to an understanding of what lives in a person.

> *If now, for example, you form for yourselves vivid meditation-images of the whole existence of what is musical in yourselves, in the will-zones of the visible, and then again of what has to do with memory in music, the existence of music memories in the image-zones of the visible—and vice versa: If you bring what ties in the memory zones of the audible into connection with what lies in the memory zones of the visible—if you assemble all these phenomena and*

form meditation-images out of them you can be sure that one force in you will be stimulated: A profound power of ingenuity that you need when facing the child you are to educate.[52]

The Elements of Music and Their Relation to the Human Being

The foundation for the removal of all obstacles for the development of a courageous and appropriate development of our life of will in adulthood depends upon the right introduction to music. The particular manner in which the musical element works into the organism of man is thus, that it eases the fluctuations of nerve activity into the stream of the breath. These reverberate upon the nerve functions. Further, the breathing rhythm interacts with the rhythms of the circulatory system, which in turn work into the rhythm of sleeping and waking. It is truly wondrous to behold and understand, through anthroposophical research, the inwardly active man-creating power of music![53]

Steiner indicates here that how a child is introduced to the world of music is vital for the development of sound volitional capacities. For this reason music is introduced right from the first grade in the Waldorf school and, most importantly, not only the talented children receive musical instruction. Each one of the various musical elements is worked with and brought to the child.

The elements of music again show a threefoldness in melody, harmony and rhythm. Melody is inwardly related to the power and capacities of thinking in the human soul, harmony is related to feeling, and rhythm to the will. If we remember that music is essentially something that unfolds in time, then we realize, as Steiner also pointed out repeatedly, that we have in melody the purest expression of music. In harmony, with the simultaneous sounding of various notes, a spatial element enters in the overlapping of several *times*. In rhythm we touch, intermittently, as it were, the hard mineral earth—a physical-material factor becomes manifest. In the measure, or beat, we are solidly connected to this hard mineral earth, upon which we only touch intermittently in rhythm. Thus beat imprisons music, chains it to the earth, and can actually not be regarded as one of the true musical elements. It is only in the element of the melody that we float and flow along, in pure expression of time.

Practically speaking, therefore, we need to permit children to experience all three elements anchored down by measure. So we shall work with pitch and melody and allow children to sing and follow the *story line* of a melody. (This is not the place to elaborate the reasons for pentatonic music in the first grade.) One of the best ways to achieve immersion into this musical story line is in the form of a dialogue between teacher and students. The teacher sings and the students listen, and then vice versa. In this way each student can concentrate on listening and is not distracted from his or her own singing by attempting to listen at the same time. Also, as Steiner points out in the above statement, it is essential that listening and doing in the area of music take place in turn, and not simultaneously.

The human figure as a whole represents the tones of a musical scale. We may use the motion of the hands in an up or down direction, even touching different parts of our body, to indicate pitch. Tone-deaf children who learn to touch the respective parts of the body by following the teacher to indicate pitch learn eventually to pitch their voices, if efforts are made over several years on a regular basis.

> *The lowest tones of the octave, any octave, involve in the first place all that ties in the limb system of the human being. Then, from about E and on to F, F sharp, G, the vibrations of the etheric body join in. Then we come to the point where the vibrations of the astral body also live in the music. And then the matter comes to a head. Having started with C, C sharp, we now come to the interval of the seventh, a region where we are brought to a standstill. The experience falters and we have need of an entirely new element. . . . We must find ourselves for the second time when we reach the octave. . . . The feeling for the octave leads us to find our own selves on a higher plane. The third interval leads us to our inner being; the octave enables us to possess ourselves, to feel ourselves once again.*[54]

Thus by going up an octave, or down it, we develop a living feeling and image for the incarnation process.

In experiencing the consonance of certain intervals, or the dissonance of others, we experience the relation of our body to our head. But we also pull something into the present that should have dissolved, force something of the future into a too early audible existence—thus creating disorder in the sequential flow of time.

A continuous battle seems to be going on in the realm of music between the forces of divine and flowing changeability and the forces that aim to lock all existence into permanency. In harmony, in the multiplicity of sound, these forces of permanency gain a small foothold. In creating harmonies we resist, as it were, the flowing of the moment, its becoming and dying. We cry out, like Faust, for the fleeting moment to remain!

For this reason, children under the age of nine should engage predominantly to make music in unison; otherwise a spatial element would enter their musical experience too soon. But after they have reached this age, it is very essential that we develop children's musicality by giving them the opportunity to assert themselves in one tone or melody over and against another person. Now that they experience themselves more consciously in the realm of space, they will develop a good feeling for relationships with others through the cultivation of rounds and making music in parts. In other words, now children need to experience themselves participating in a multiplicity and diversity of sound.

In rhythm, we face a different challenge. Here we find a cyclical change between the perceptible and the non-perceptible, the pause. Here, we knock against the physical reality with every beat; we dissolve it with every pause. What a clear indication this is that we have to deal here with the will element in individuals! It is the will—in a sense this most spiritual of human soul forces and akin to the eternal self—which takes hold of the most earthly and material objects and forms them. Our limbs are intimately concerned with the bringing forth of rhythms. We stamp, we clap, we knock on various sound-producing instruments. We repeatedly and cyclically confront material existence. Within us the rhythm of heartbeat and breath is the most easily observed, although many other body rhythms work intimately into our existence. Rhythm, though, is flexible and varied; beat—measure—is monotone repetition. When rhythm becomes too inflexible, it really is made too earthy and turns into beat.

To remind ourselves again of the twofold ego experience in music, and of the fact that music is the working of the ego forces into the forces of man's astral body, we must understand that the natural progression in the realm of music enters from two sides: from the head with the melody and from the limbs with rhythm. By and by we then approach also the conscious work with harmony and the intervals.

Temperaments and the Three Elements of Music

Superficially speaking, one could describe the melodious element itself as tending more towards the melancholic, the harmonious element towards the sanguine and phlegmatic modes, and the choleric element working through the rhythms.

This is an approppriate place to refer to Steiner's correlation of the musical instruments with the temperaments, as suggested in his *Discussions with Teachers* (Anthroposophic Press, Hudson, NY, 1997, GA 295, Lecture of August 21, 1919). He indicates that the piano—otherwise not a *real* instrument—could be used for phlegmatics, the wind instruments for sanguine children, the percussion instruments for the cholerics, and voice, especially solo, for the melancholics. It is noted that all children are predominantly sanguine, and so it follows that all should learn the recorder first, as is done in practice in Waldorf schools. Anyone who has taught music with knowledge of the temperaments knows how important it is for the cholerics to have the opportunity to use percussion instruments.

The melancholics tend to respond also very well to string instruments, such as the violin, for in being able to play such an instrument, the deep melancholy of the soul can pour itself into music, and jubilant song may free the soul of its woes. Indeed, for melancholics to play an instrument that lends itself to pure melody, such as violin or flute, is important. Wind instruments, on the other hand, already tend towards the Dionysian, and thus are generally more suitable for sanguines.

Of course we must realize that any indications are only indications and that there are many individual differences. Moreover, within melody itself there is a threefoldness, within harmony and the intervals of a scale another threefoldness, and within the field of rhythm yet another threefold distinction which must be made. Melodies may flow monotonously along the same pitch, they can rise upwards in pitch, or they can sink. Thus melody may tend towards the head, down towards the limbs, or remain level within the middle region.

Harmonies do the same thing in terms of intervals: Fourths and fifths hold the middle position, tonic through third holds the lower, the limb position, and sixths, sevenths, and octaves tend towards the head.

Rhythms couch this whole threefold aspect of the human being into a different form: The stress on the first foot of the rhythm, as it were, puts a little *head* there, making it topheavy; the stress on the last foot, towards the end, and even more so if there is a syncopated rhythm, introduces a limb quality; and the monotone, as well as the stress in the middle of a rhythm, holds a balance.

In his *Eurythmy as Visible Music*,[56] Steiner relates very clearly how threefold space—the vertical, horizontal and sagittal directions—is related to pitch, beat and rhythm. The whole human form represents all elements of music. Thus when an individual moves, all elements of music may be made manifest spatially and, as it were, coaxed out of him into space. If we now remember what we have indicated earlier about the working of the polarity of the contractive and expansive forces regarding the three dimensions of space, we can get a clearer picture of the differentiation on each plane. This diagram shows a little the inner relationship between sculpture, movement and music:

Let us now summarize the activity of the temperaments in the three areas of music:

In the realm of melody, the scale from high to low tones expresses the range from the melancholic to the choleric as it goes from the contractive high voice to the expansive low one.

In harmony we find the same range of the scale but now in terms of intervals. Now we have the interrelationship of the contractive and the expansive elements: Head and limbs both play parts simultaneously.

In the field of rhythm we are concerned with the following: Looking at the human form anatomically, we may perceive a progression from the unit of the head—as one rounded form of closely knit and integrated skull bones—to the more dispersed and differentiated bones of arm, leg, hand and foot. This is a progression from unity to diversity. In the head region rhythm is fettered into solid rest; the melancholic is unrhythmical for this reason—consolidation is predominant. In the limb region rhythm is dissolved, it is whisked out of existence before it is born—the choleric is often too erratic for a rhythm to develop. Cholerics are rhythmical when they are challenged to be so, not so much by natural inclination. In the middle region rhythm may live: a little more monotonously, and a little closer to the head in the phlegmatic, a little more *dancingly* and closer to the limbs in the sanguine.

The stress of each rhythm will tell us to which region it belongs. A stress on the first foot emphasizes the head, a stress on the last, the limb nature.

At this point something else needs to be considered: Actual awareness of the temperaments, and their working, in the field of the music lessons is not necessarily important. The musical element is in itself so permeated by living weaving cosmic musicality that any good musician will instinctively work in the different temperament modes: They are inherent in music. But what *is* really important is that musicality should permeate all areas of teaching. In this way life-giving musicality aids the teacher to develop a relationship with his or her class and with the individual child—a relationship that is enlivened by the dynamics of the temperaments in action. Steiner makes it quite clear that all arts need to be inspired by music in order to remain sources of artistic creativity.

> *Now in the course of the history of art there existed a general movement which tended more to the plastic or graphic arts. Today we must again inject new life into the plastic arts, for the immediacy of the original impulse was lost years ago. For centuries the impulse towards music has been growing and expanding. Therefore the plastic arts have assumed a musical character to a greater or lesser extent. Music, which includes also the musical element in the arts of speech, is destined to be the art of the future.*
> *The first Goetheanum at Dornach was conceived musically and for this reason its architecture, sculpture and painting met with so little understanding. And for the same reason, the second Goetheanum will also meet with little understanding because the element of music must be introduced into painting, sculpture and architecture, in accordance with man's future evolution.*[56]

If we take Steiner's remark seriously, we need to seek ways and means of permeating all arts, and therefore all teaching, with musical elements, instead of having only actual music and singing itself. Let it be understood that actual music instruction and a good deal of singing are essential. But let it be also understood, that when talking about the temperaments in relation to music, we have the possibility to come to an understanding of the actual musical element. Conversely, musicality itself is a key to an understanding of the essence of temperament character and activity.

Before we look again at the human being in terms of the elements of music, we need to make a few more remarks about different types of music in relation to the polarity of forces.

The Polarizing Powers and Music

One of Steiner's characterizations of the luciferic and the ahrimanic profiles is that the former is inclined to prolong and proliferate earlier stages of development, earlier historical periods into the present time, and also to allow the influences of youth to linger longer in an individual, than would normally be the case. The latter, on the other hand, is inclined to hurry individuals on into the future, into coming periods of development, to introduce into the present time what would really be appropriate only at a later date. Thus the ahrimanic impulse is one to speed up what lives in the present and usher in the future prematurely, whereas the luciferic impulse is to delay development and prolong the influences of the past. Moreover, the luciferic impulse tends to bring spiritual substance down into the physical, and the ahrimanic impulse attempts to bring material substance into the spiritual realm.

From this viewpoint we may begin to understand several tendencies in contemporary music. An increasing polarization of the luciferic and ahrimanic took place towards the end of the last century. We note that the Romantic composers—Romanticism exhibits a tendency towards the luciferic—were on the increase. On the other hand, we find the tendency to mechanize music, to fragment it through the use of technology, an ahrimanic inspiration. Musical compositions that imitate nature have also such an impulse. Computer music is a further atomization of the being of music.

A more hidden aspect of the ahrimanic intentions for our time, as Steiner points out in several of his lectures, is this. One of Ahriman's impulses is to lead individuals into instinctive spiritual vision and clair-

voyance. Human beings will again be able to see into the spiritual worlds—
this is a prospect for humanity, which appears sporadically in our time,
and will increase in the future. Ahriman attempts to push this tendency
into our present time, so that individuals instinctively and possibly, too
soon, may become clairvoyant. Steiner hints that ahrimanic methods will
be used—and do we not see evidence enough already—to teach men quick
ways to look into the spiritual worlds. There is a certain type of music
purporting to be spiritual, and often using all the gimmicks of electronic
gadgetry, which could be perceived as leading individuals into a pseudo-
spiritual experience.

    The human being himself, though, is formed out of heavenly
music. We may see the relation to the musical elements in this way:

Music-Permeated Teaching—the Art of Relevant Presentation

    To add yet another controversial statement to these pages, one
could say that teaching becomes an art in as far as it is permeated by
musicality. Before describing an example of how musicality can permeate
teaching, let me make a few introductory remarks.

    As stated above, permeating one's teaching with musicality is not
the same as permeating it with music. I do not mean to suggest that to
seek out songs and pieces of music which one regards as suitable, and
bring them to students, is an irrelevant interlude before getting on with
the subject matter. Yet another level of permeation is meant: To infuse the
subject matter with artistic experiences and activities which are relevant
to the conceptual contents, and which are interspersed *musically*, that is,

in the manner of a theme and its variations, into the whole course of the lessons. In this way we may make all details, all facets, relevant to the whole. Elements of music may be part of such an activity or not, but the various facets comprising a learning experience need to sound together like the parts of a piece of music.

This means also that as a teacher—as I have attempted to indicate above—one strives to so deepen one's understanding of the essence of each major conceptual content, so that one is able to translate it into the visual, the sculptural, the musical elements, or into dramatic movement and gesture. We can only perform this difficult transformation by means of what Steiner calls active thinking, as opposed to the ordinary passive thinking concerned with an intellectual view of the world.

> *Hence you find in my 'Philosophy of Spiritual Activity'* [Intuitive Thinking as a Spiritual Path, Anthroposophic Press, Hudson, NY, 1995] *an exposition on the art of forming concepts, a description of what takes place in the soul when one does not keep with one's concepts to the impressions from the outside, but lives within the free flow of thoughts. That, my dear friends, is an activity which aims at knowledge in a far deeper sense than the external knowledge of Nature, but it is at the same time artistic, wholly identical with artistic activity. So that the moment pure thinking is experienced as will, man's attitude becomes that of an artist.*[58]

If we strive in the way indicated, we can present a relevant and cohesive learning experience to the child in which conceptual and artistic -sensory as well as feeling aspects of any subject are integrated because they prove themselves to be variations on one theme. When attempting to work in this way, temperament language—as pointed out in Chapter 2—is the agent of transformation of concepts, derived through active thinking, into an artistic form.

The relationship of the temperaments to music thus actually reveals itself in two ways. One is the concrete relationship of the different components of music—rhythm, harmony and melody; also the quality of the different instruments to the four temperaments belongs to this direct relation to music. The other is that any unfolding process demonstrates the dynamics of the interplay of the temperaments as pure, or intangible music—for it takes place in the medium of time.

As I hinted above (see Chapter 4), the creative process is a process demonstrating temperament dynamics—that is, the weaving of the four seasons of creation. In as far as any lesson is a whole, this whole comes about through the dynamics of a course of events, musicality permeating and differentiating the very flow of time. A fundamentally musical current enlivens the unfolding of any event.

Thus it is vital to realize that in a musical sequence whatever is later in time influences the former. In the flow of the lesson, specifically, the main concept that is to arise clearly at the end already influences the steps which are to be taken towards that end—the future already intones the closing chord in the present—musically speaking.

A side remark: The steps towards an end are relevant to this end, not irrelevant. Steiner's repeated warning should be remembered here, that Ahriman is behind every means which is not inherently relevant—and therefore true—to the end which it is meant to serve. Education today, which is influenced strongly by behaviorist philosophy, shows irrelevant, and thus inherently untrue, use of means to achieve an educational end. One might call this the hidden immorality of much of present day educational indoctrination.

The Morphology of Europe—Introduced Musically

When we introduce the geography of what might be the first distant continent (for North American students) the starting point has to be a morphological one. As the morphological features of Europe are more complex than those of any other continent, a framework for the morphology needs to be established. Europe with its many peninsulas, its very intimate interpenetration of land and sea, has a complex coastline. The mountains are the skeletons, the seas and rivers the surging, moving, rhythmic blood and vascular system of this being called Europe. We shall attempt to describe how the major features of the morphology in terms of mountains and waters can be translated into musical/dramatic action.

Scene I

The class is divided into two groups: One will act as the mountains, the other at first the seas, later the rivers. The mountain group stands in the center of the room and chants/sings words somewhat like the following: "We are the mountains tall and strong." The music could be somewhat like this:

As the children sing, they gesture, raising their arms over their heads to indicate pitch, height of mountains, and maybe also stamp in time with the words.

At the same time the second group has formed into a circle around the mountain group and chants/sings: "Wind and water on the shores, ever moving waves are we."

These two groups move, respectively, more or less in the center and on the circumference of a circle. The mountain group stands and gestures on the spot, the water group moves along the circumference circling the other. Gradually, the teacher will lead the water group into a wave line, becoming more and more pronounced, drawing nearer to the mountains, or receding to the periphery in rhythmic motion. A kind of dialogue of movement ensues between these two groups, all the time accompanied by the singing/chanting, as well as suitable gestures with the arms. Harmonious interaction between these two groups is essential.

Scene II

The mountain group will now diversify, splitting up into smaller groups. Each group will become one of the major mountainous ranges and complexes of Europe and place themselves in their relative positions, as if the floor were a map of Europe. One by one they tell and sing who they are, until in the end the several voices join together: "We are the mountains tall and strong. We are the Alps from East to West. We are the Apennines to the South. We are the Pyrenees to the Southwest. We are the Carpathians to the East" and so forth. The splitting up occurs during the singing, and each group keeps moving, gesturing, singing on the spot, representing the map of Europe.

The seas here accompany the mountains with gently swelling motions. Now it is time again for them to move. The walking of the waves becomes more and more dramatic, as gradually they walk the shape of Europe's coastline. Now, on the outside of the circle, the seas might separate and form their own bodies of water: "Wind and water on the shore, ever moving waves are we: The North Sea, the Gulf of Biscay, the English Channel, the Mediterranean Sea, the Baltic Sea, the Black Sea," and so forth.

Again, we shall seek to let the music underline the very picture of the many water bodies surrounding the mountains. The aim is to get the class to experience the formative forces of the morphology, from the whole to the differentiated parts, out of the interplay of the two polarities—earthy mountains and watery oceans, the fixed and the mobile.

Scene III

One further possible step is to let the course of Europe's principal rivers arise out of the implicit tension of the polarity of mountains and seas as a third, mercurially uniting element. Individual students may wind their way landwards portraying the course of the Rivers Rhine, Rhone, Danube, Volga, and so on. Implicit in this dramatic action is also the nature of the cultural role of the big waterways—their role of facilitating communication and commerce between human beings. Seas and mountains may separate individuals and nations, but the mercurial rivers help them communicate.

The *river children* might sing: "I am the (name of river). I roll upstream to my source, from coastal plains to mighty towering crag."

The choreography of such a *geography opera* for the three scenes would be somewhat like this:

Once we have performed it daily for about a week, the students are ready to translate their spatial experience into a map. A good sequence is to paint first, then draw, and finally model it in clay or wax.

As we move further into geography, we may characterize the different parts of Europe and its many peoples directly in terms of music. Now, instead of being mountain ranges and rivers, groups of students could represent the different parts of Europe: Northern Europe, Eastern Europe, Southern Europe, and so forth. This gives ample opportunity for the enterprising class teacher to compose music expressing the character of the people in these different parts of Europe: The Southern Latin temperament—vivaciously sanguine, and even tinged a little by the fiery choleric; the melancholic Northern, in minor mode; the watery/phlegmatic Western, and the bouncy-folksy central European, most balanced of all. Not to forget the Russian, combining the choleric with the melancholic, as is apparent in so many Russian folk songs.

In such a way we would arouse in our students a real feeling for the nature of the peoples of Europe, for their connection to their very earth and landscape—and this is what geography is all about. Indeed, Steiner emphasized the importance of geography teaching by indicating that it is vital for the development of healthy social impulses for later life.

The dramatization of the morphology of Europe as enacted by students already carries within it an inner visualization of the map of Europe. By juxtaposing events which dramatize this map—in gesture, gestalt, in tonality, in visual image, we bring its various facets closer to the student. This example shows both direct and indirect working with the musical elements: direct, because actual musical themes are sung and performed; indirect, because the dramatic build-up of these scenes unfolds musically.

The musical flow is the mother lode out of which—in the end—conceptual knowledge crystallizes. A sequence of experiences and activities, which are inherently relevant to the final concept comes about if we permeate teaching with musicality. We are teaching that each step contains the whole, however hidden, as each part of a plant contains potentially the whole plant. So we build the foundation for living concepts. Relevancy is relatedness on a deeper level than the temperament/element level. A new dimension appears to have been added. Without the foundation of the temperament correspondence in cosmic and human existence, however, we shall also not find the key to present relevant factors.

The starting point to the above example was the inherent contrast between earth and water. Our knowledge of their incisive characteristics enabled us to develop them dramatically. This musical dramatization revealed the inherent dynamics. The mode of experience was relevant to the subject.

Chapter Seven

Language, Art and Temperament

Imagine that we have here the expired air, on which are impressed certain words that the human being speaks. Whilst this breath, formed into words, streams outwards from the breast, the rhythmic vibration goes downward and passes over into the whole watery element that permeates the human organism. Thus at the level of his throat, his speech-organs, man has the air-rhythms when he speaks. But along with his speaking goes a wave-like surging and seething of the whole fluid-body in the human being. The fluid in man that is below the region of speech comes into vibration and vibrates in harmony. This is what it really means when we say that our speech is accompanied by feelings. If the watery element in the human being did not vibrate in harmony in this way, man's speech would go forth from him neutrally, indifferently; he would not be able to permeate what he says with feeling. And upwards in the direction of the head goes the element of warmth, and accompanying the words that we impress upon the air are upward-streaming waves of warmth, which permeate the head and there make it possible for our words to be accompanied by thought.[59]

— Rudolf Steiner

In language individuals recreate themselves. They send out words on a stream of air, having fashioned each word by uniting the formative consonant stream with the feeling vowel stream. Thus, in language we have a unique form of unification of the two polarities as they act in each individual. Moreover, it is apparent that in every word, sentence and speech which an individual sends out into the world, he or she lives in the stream of time, as is also the case when one is engaged with music. Speech has as its lowest physical basis the waves (vibrations) of air. Within a person the fluid organization vibrates with it, resonates, when speaking. We sculpt the element of air, of light, while speaking and endow it with thought in as far as we let our warmth flow into it. The astral nature on the waves of the air forms the vowels, and the etheric forms resonating within a person form the consonants.

We have in the very physiology and morphology of speech an indication of how language comes into being in the intangible zone between astral and etheric, streamed through by human ego warmth and thought contents. Thus it may be obvious that in the very sounds of language we would find the working of the temperament/element modes. We shall return to this in greater detail, but let it be noted now that vowel sounds are carriers of the expansive polarity and consonants of the contractive. This is, of course, a generalization, for within each of the ranges of the vowels, as well as the consonants, there is also the spectrum from the expansive to the contractive.

I have been able to give language here only the sketchiest of treatments, and from only one point of view, though it is hoped that the reader will feel challenged to follow each hint with her or his own elaborations.

The Structure of Language

One of the secrets inherent in language is that in each facet of the spoken word, the whole human being is contained. In each word itself there is the threefoldness of body—the actual air body of the word; of soul—that is musicality, pitch, tonality and coloration, which carries all the emotional and feeling overtones, as it were; and of spirit—the conceptual contents, the thought lightly incarnated into it through warmth.

Considering each sentence, we find a similar wholeness reflecting the essence of what is human. Each sentence has a head—the subject, which is expressed by a noun or a noun phrase; it has a limb-metabolic system—the predicate that is expressed by the main verb with its object. And further, the body may be extended in various directions with a variety of subsidiary clauses. The simplest sentence already shows the basic polarity of head and body.

I would suggest further—and this is far more difficult both to illustrate and to prove—that each piece of writing, each story, drama, essay and so forth, can be seen as a whole, showing the basic human triad of incarnation if we were but sufficiently subtle in our observation. Possibly one could call this triad structure (of the body), character (of the soul), and contents (of the spirit).

Each sentence may be compared to a miniature human being. The parts of speech in a sentence are related to each other in the same way as the different parts of the body are related to the whole person. With every sentence we utter, we send an *air person* into our surroundings. The noun of a simple sentence is its head, the verb its limbs, the adjective its heart, and the adverb is its digestive system. Or, to include other parts of speech, one may see the adjective in the right arm, the adverb in the left arm, the verb in the right leg, the preposition in the left leg. Small wonder that even young children in the process of learning to speak know instinctively how to round out the wholeness of the sentence. As infants they have been learning to explore their own movement system, too. Small wonder that the instinct for this *deep structure* of language, to use Noam Chomsky's term, seems inborn: Children know as instinctively, not intellectually, of course, what constitutes a wholeness of meaning as they know the completeness of their own body.

Another extraordinary facet of language is the fact that one aims at the completion of a sentence while still speaking it—thus language actually runs ahead of thought. Just think of what we express often inadvertently with our repartee without having given careful consideration to what we thus express. To phrase this another way: Conscious and deliberate thinking seems slower and more cumbersome compared to the lightning swift instinctive thought expressed in the immediacy of language. Something related to our language capacity runs ahead of us, as it were, and works in from the future so that we aim the sentence towards its conclusion. This is a vital facet of our language.

Speech, like music, flows with time, flows in from the future through our inherent, and instinctively wise, capacity to resolve and complete a trend of thought, a sentence. But unlike the sounds of music, speech sounds carry further differentiation.

> *When we hear an 'a' or an 'i' or other sounds, a subconscious activity momentarily transforms a melody into a harmony. That is the secret of sound; it is melody transformed into harmony. This marvellous subconscious activity proceeds in approximately the same way as the various refractions in the eye are carried out according to physical laws, which is another process we can call to consciousness after it has taken place.*[60]

A further question arises: What is the organ in us, which enables us to understand the meaning of another person's words?

We would not be able to understand words did we not possess a physical movement organism. Truly, within the nerves leading from the central nervous system to our total movement organism is contained the sensory organ for the perception of words spoken to us. Thus are the sense organs specialized: The whole man—sense organ for the perception of the ego, the self of another man; the life organization underlying the physical organization—sense organ for the perception of thought; the independently mobile man—sense organ for the perception of words.[61]

The above statement is of immense importance for teachers. Steiner confirms here that the sense organ for the comprehension of the spoken word of another person is our entire movement organization—our whole body in as far we are able to move. As teachers we come to realize that unless the bodily movement of children is fostered and developed in a healthy way, they will not be able to understand their fellow human beings. One element of human communication is thus intrinsically dependent on the child's ability to move. One is reminded here of the efforts of child psychologists who developed movement exercises for the therapeutic treatment of a variety of dyslexic conditions, then termed aphasias, several decades ago.

Conclusion, Judgment, Concept

Here we need to make a further exploration into the depths of the human being in order to better understand the deeper structure of language as it serves the expression of thought. Three faculties ascribed to logical thinking are vital for intelligent communication between human beings: The faculties to *arrive* at conclusions, *make* judgments, and *form* concepts. (Note the genius of language choosing these three verbs to fit these three faculties.)

How children learn to develop these three faculties, leading to logical thinking, is a vital question for the elementary school teacher, for it is during the elementary school age that children need to develop them gradually. Steiner refers to it in depth in his *Foundations of Human Expe-*

rience (op. cit., Lecture of August 29, 1919). Here he states that, contrary to prevailing assumptions,

> *[t]he first thing you form is a conclusion; the second is a judgment; the last thing you come to in life is a concept. Of course you are not aware that you are continuously carrying out this activity; but it is only by means of this activity that you can lead a conscious life which enables you to communicate with other human beings through speech. It is commonly thought that one comes to concepts first of all. That is not true.*

Steiner points out, too, that each sentence is already a judgment. Concepts are most deeply inserted into the human being. The sleeping soul itself inserts concepts into the being of the child. Teachers, he exhorts, should refrain from bringing finished concepts to the child. Such finished concepts act as dead, inert bodies, which are indigestible to the soul. He also indicates a way to awaken a child's thought potential.

> *You must treat a child of this kind (a dullard) by building as little as possible on his powers of knowing, on his understanding, but by 'hammering' in some things which will work strongly on the will, by letting him walk while he speaks.*[62]

There is a further indication of the intimate relationship of language with the movement of the whole body.

> *Only representation as such is really a matter of the head activity. In making a judgment, you need to sense, via the mediation of the etheric body, the way in which you stand with your legs, for you do not judge with your head at all, but with your legs, respectively with your etheric legs. Whoever makes judgments when lying down simply stretches forth his etheric legs. Making judgments is a matter for the legs, not of the head! Of course no one believes this, though it is true. The arriving at conclusions also rests upon the arms and the legs; actually upon all that man has which raises*

him beyond the animal. An animal also uses its legs; the animal itself is a judgment, but it does not arrive at conclusions. Man makes conclusions, for this reason he has arms, not for walking. Man has arms which can move freely, so that he is able to arrive at conclusions. That which happens when man stretches forth his ether legs and his astral arms in judgment, in conclusion, that is reflected only in the head as representation and thus becomes concept. Thus one makes use of complete man, not only nerve-sensory man, to make judgments and arrive at conclusions.[63]

We have gone this circuitous route in order to get a feeling for a person's complete involvement in all aspects of the being and structure of language. The human essence of physical movement is thus fundamentally concerned with endowing an individual with the faculty to express himself or herself intelligently and communicate with his fellow man, as likewise the movement in an individual's own astral and etheric bodies provides the foundation for understanding and thinking.

Let us remind ourselves here that the art of painting works from the astral forces into the etheric nexus of forces and the art of music from the ego into the astral realm. With this we have one clue why artistic activity as part of teaching fosters the learning process, for we come to a conclusion musically; we arrive at a judgment pictorially.

Comparison between Rudolf Steiner's presentation of the stages of
logical thinking in two of his works:

Foundations of Human Experience
1919
Sleeping Soul

Waking Soul: does not
work on the body

Dreaming Soul: Feeling

Therapeutic Insights
1921
Reflection in head:
representation
and concept

Conclusion: astral
arms and legs

Judgment: etheric
legs and feet

Remembering here the concept of the essential self of each individual, of the outer and inner ego, both of which are in such heavenly balance in music, we can arrive at the conclusion that in speech the outer ego is predominant. Indeed,

> [i]f we go on to speak about the higher members of the human beings, starting with the spirit-self, we can refer to them only as something which is still outside the human being. For, in this fifth post-Atlantean epoch, we are only just beginning to make this spirit-self one of our inner members. But if we accept it as a gift from a higher sphere and sink it into our ego, taking with us what as yet can only be dimly felt of the spirit-self, then poetry is born.[64]

The Muse of Poetry engages the self in the divine dance of the gods so that inspired words would reach not only earthly conclusions but also heavenly ones moistened by the dew of revelation. Thus a deep musicality is active in the time element of language, in its structure, in its very sounds as the stream of words is modified and differentiated into sentences, into rhymes and rhythms.

One more remark about language before going on to its relation to the temperaments. To the degree that our movement capacity, through the interference of technology, becomes rigid and limited, an individual's language ability is also damaged and with it her or his ability to think logically. These effects are already apparent in present-day children. We have, therefore, a vital task in the field of the language arts, which can contribute to healing some of the damage which present-day civilization has inflicted upon the young.

When concerning ourselves thus with the connection of language structure to the human being, it is obvious that we must tread the following path: We begin with addressing the conscious soul life, within which lives the faculty for drawing conclusions in the middle realm of the human being; then we lead this over into the realm of the dreaming soul, thus effecting judgment with the help of our feet; finally we shall allow the sleeping soul to work during actual sleep, or during a period of *forgetting*, to form the concepts which are reflected in the head. Compare this with the above diagram and also with the key picture of the learning process as described in Chapter 2.

The above sequence may form a basis for arriving at a process of teaching in concordance with an individual's spiritual being: From the musicality of the middle part of the human physiology we then enter the spatial-formative element by moving our feet over the ground. This movement activity then becomes transformed into the conceptual and image quality, which is typical of the head region. The whole human being is thus active in the transformation of conclusion into judgment and on into concept.

Temperament and the Teaching of Language Arts

Let us remind ourselves of the three stages of language development as characterized in Chapter 2. In all three stages, in all three areas of expression—gesture and movement, rhythm and musicality, image and concept—we have the possibility of differentiation according to temperament, for we may bring the fiery, airy, watery and earthy elements right into all these forms of language expression. If we now correlate what has been suggested in the preceding chapters with the development of language, we may arrive at the following possibility for both grasping and developing the teaching of language arts, as it teaches expression of our essential being, in three steps.

Firstly, we would engage children in the area of conclusion, the area of musicality and rhythm of language in the rhythmic region of the body, which is also the second stage of the development of language in human evolution. We would then foster speech and dramatic action at this point. It would also be imperative to let students move their arms in flowing motion together with the spoken word. Intonation and gesture would be colored by the different temperament modalities according to the four elements. In the art of speech formation we nurture the confluence of voice and gesture. All the recitation and drama work done in Waldorf classrooms from first grade on serves to establish this natural and artistic immersion into the element of the spoken word. It also serves to counteract the mundane element of everyday language.

As a second step we would carry this over into spatial movements and patterns, which we express through the choreography of our steps on the ground, thus involving feet and legs to accompany words and sentences meaningfully.

We should not miss the opportunity of giving the child what one could call a spatial picture of a main and a relative clause. Naturally this can be done in the most varied ways. Without wanting to theorize one could represent the main clause as a large circle and the relative clause as a small one, perhaps an concentric circle. The conditional clause, the 'if-sentence,' could now be shown by lines drawn towards the circle like rays indicating the conditioning factors... It is really necessary, after appropriate preparation of one's material, to come back to these matters again and again, and even with ten, eleven, twelve year olds to go into the moral-characterological aspect of style made visible by pictures. This does not imply teaching syntax, for the pupil should grasp these matters in a more intuitive way. One can really go a long way here. For instance one can introduce a short story from the point of view of the temperaments, having thoroughly prepared it beforehand.[65]

The most significant point here is the spatial representation of language through which an inner sense for structure is awakened in the child. The different form principles inherent in the temperament modes show themselves here in the contractive-circular or the expansive-radial gesture of the form, as well as in our orientation and direction.

Thirdly, we advance to an image, which is redolent with meaning, with contents, with concept. In the image, in the pictorial, we have yet another possibility to infuse meaning by temperament mode: by evoking visual and audible contour, color, and shape in an earthy, fiery, airy, and watery modulation.

Example: Subject and Predicate

The introduction of subject and predicate is indicated for the fifth grade. We take, for example, the following sentence through all three stages: Pallas Athena sprang forth from Zeus' forehead.

The first day: We would speak the sentence with a distinctive caesura between the subject—Pallas Athena—and the predicate with the object—sprang forth from Zeus's forehead. Accompanying the words, we would make a rounded gesture with our hands, a little head, as it were, when speaking the subject, and then let a long, horizontal gesture accompany the rest of the sentence. We use here spherical and radial forms. Our intonation would adapt itself to the gesture.

The second day: We would challenge the class to show us how we could walk this sentence on the floor such that the difference between these two parts of the sentence is apparent. This may be done with classes which have been used to the spatial representation of sentences since second grade. Otherwise a lengthier introduction may be needed. With a little coaching, the class could arrive at something like this: To stand still in the center while speaking the subject and to move around the center along the periphery swiftly while speaking the predicate. It should be noted that in this arrangement, when the verb is spoken, the person in the middle jumps out from the center to the periphery—the most active motion of the whole sentence.

The third day: We would now draw and write what has been enacted before. The sentence now becomes entirely visual, and with it, through repeated practice, conceptual. The children now know the division of a sentence into subject and predicate—and will eventually be able to characterize this difference verbally.

We have followed a path from the middle realm of the human body—where the organ of speech is situated, and linked it with gesture, as the fourfold temperament mode shows itself in both. In the above example the subject will be mainly melancholic and the predicate choleric and sanguine. The contractive element in gesture and motion is here quite tangible, as is the expansive when we let it sink down into the patterns walked by our feet. With the latter we have let it sink down into the second area, the area of judgment. Finally, we let the image crystallize and be reflected conceptually in the head. This three-day procedure is one of the principles of transformation as suggested by Steiner at various times, so that the subject to be learned may be experienced in a living way by each student.

It is important to point out once more that we have begun this process with the second stage of language development because we need to begin with that which is *present*, with that which is factual, with that which is whole, before moving into analysis.

The Three-Day Process

When discussing the teaching of physics, Steiner describes in detail the learning process as it takes place over three days.[66] He also applies this process to the teaching of history. I would suggest that in other subjects a similar process may be adopted and be found helpful, although one would not separate the various stages rigidly, but let them evolve organically. Let me emphasize that by following this three-day procedure, we begin with the musical/rhythmical/vocal facets of the subject matter. Then we transform them into actual spatial motion over the ground in choreographed movement. Finally we allow them to crystallize into an image/concept. As Steiner indicates in the above named lecture, by spreading out this process over three days, we work from the ego/astral/day-consciousness pole into the astral/etheric/dream nature of our being, and finally into the etheric/physical/form structure. There we are least conscious, but now it becomes part of memory, and so becomes our mental property. In this way we are constantly engaged in building up our inner world, and this process—spread out over three days—aids the assimilation of knowledge which is most appropriate to a human being's inner, spiritual and soul nature.

Style, Temperament and Rhythm

We now need to relate the temperaments to the three great sections of language as an art: epic, dramatic, and lyrical poetry. The question of creative writing and style should also concern us here.

Each of the three great sections of poetic language can, for instance, be correlated to one of the kings in Goethe's fairytale of the *Green Snake and the Beautiful Lily*. Epos is the golden king; lyrical poetry the silver king; drama is the iron king. All other writing may be related to the mixed king—as all possible forms of style are mixed.

The head nature of an epic style is apparent. Well-rounded, formed sentences roll in majestic array—whether in verse or prose—to unfold a panorama of the past. The landscape of historic and mythological imagery unfolds here. Epos is mythological. It is apparent that the contractive rather than the expansive polarity dominates in epos, in narrative, and the unfolding of historical description. The great epics engender thoughtfulness. Thus the melancholic and phlegmatic temperaments contribute especially to the epic style.

It is a different matter where dramatic style is concerned. Dialogue is polarization, juxtaposition and interaction, give and take. Language itself becomes the carrier of action here. Dramatic confrontation of characters pulls the observer into the time span enacted in the drama and thus into the immediacy of the present action. The impact of its immediacy instantly involves the spectator—a sign of good drama—so that he or she becomes a participant and witness of action. In drama we have probably the Mars quality of language expressed to its fullest.

The choleric temperament is closely related to the spirit of drama itself. Clearly, though, despite an overlying choleric mood, each of the temperaments must be represented as the actor's characterization of his part demands. Steiner gives very precise indications in *Speech and Drama* about how actors should prepare themselves to act the different temperaments on the stage.[67]

Lyrical poetry holds an intermediate position: airy or watery, as the case may be. Rhythmic equilibrium between the two other styles reveals itself here. Here, also, is the most natural application of rhyme and meter, though the poetic rhythms often play a vital part in the other styles. The airy and watery reflect the world of semblance ruled by the silver king. Indeed, the truly poetical element hovers on the edge of reality, throwing its many-colored mantle over everything conceptual. It touches outer reality but lightly, yet promises the greatest of revelations, which seem to reach out from the future into the present to tug at our very heartstrings. Thus true poetry emerges as conversation with the future, with the realm of possibility.

All four elements are traceable in the poetic form, rhythm and usage of speech sounds. In the very usage of poetic rhythms we may discover that a work of poetry tends towards the epic, in the broad hexameters, for instance, which swell and roll in panorama; or the dramatic/cholerically forceful and tersely apt characterization of many a poem which carries great power of thought or action within it. In the lively and rippling rhythms of the lyrical we find the true heart of poetry in all shades from the whimsical to the profound—here the sanguine/phlegmatic temperaments show their formative action in mercurial sequence of coagulation and dissolution. I leave the task of examples to the reader.

The four great meters—iambus, anapest, dactyl and trochee—may be thought of corresponding to the four temperament modes. Iambus and anapest, having the accent at the end, tend toward the expansive polarity, and thus are related to the choleric and the sanguine respectively; dactyl and trochee, beginning with the accent—which holds them back—correspond to the contractive phlegmatic and melancholic modes.

As a class teacher we shall acquaint all students with all three styles of poetic language through our own presentation and their participation by the telling and retelling of stories; by pantomime or dramatic presentation and performance; and by reciting poetry in chorus and individually. In such ways also the greatest of artists will become familiar to the students. Further, and this is of extreme importance, we shall help children to do their own creative writing in all three styles.

The writing of stories, usually in the form of retelling what has been heard in class, is the first of the areas into which children grow naturally in the Waldorf approach. The stories told in the first four grades offer abundant material for retelling and thus for introducing the epic element of language. While introducing students to this task, it is essential to spend some time discussing the contents of what needs to be written in order to establish a mood every time we ask a class to write. Further, it is very helpful if certain elements, such as sequence of events, and spelling of names, and so forth, are discussed first and clarified, so that students enter into this activity with a certain amount of reassurance. This approach follows, once we understand why we need to begin with the present, the realm of feeling, the middle realm of human experience, as indicated above—that is, the model of the key stages of the learning process as described in Chapter 2.

The writing of poetry can easily be encouraged from around the ninth year on. It simply reflects a growing awareness of the musicality of language and builds upon the natural musicality of the child. After several years of speaking poetry in such a way that the rhythmical/musical character is stressed, with a little encouragement simple poetic forms appear to come naturally to many children. By attempting to write poetry, children hone their feeling for rhyme and rhythm, for the musicality of language altogether. Naturally the intricacies of poetic meters and forms need not be entered into more seriously for several years. This is actually study material in the Waldorf high school.

The language arts block usually referred to as *Wish-Wonder-Surprise* in the seventh grade offers the possibility to discuss differences in style in far greater depth than was possible before. One of the important distinctions we shall have to make with the students, will be between the actual/factual and the potential/possible through developing the sensitivity for the subtle shades of meaning conveyed by the different moods of the verb.

These finer gradations of meaning and language are, when well studied and practiced with seventh graders, an essential experience in preparation for the emotional storms of puberty. It is of value for pre-puberty students to learn to distinguish between the actual and the wishful, the imaginary and the factual, for this is one of the treacherous cliffs they will have to learn to circumnavigate in the course of the next few years. The dramatic element, too, begins to come into its own from the ninth, tenth year on. This is an age that heralds individual awakening and thus is particularly suitable for dramatic expression.

A side remark: Who as a teacher has not encountered the child who uses impudent and insolent intonation at times when addressing an adult, but who is apparently completely unaware of its inappropriateness? Active dramatic work brings this into awareness and thus eventually under control.

It is also good to foster impromptu dramatic scenes in the last years of the elementary school. In this way the students are challenged to employ awareness of themselves and learn to tune voice, language, tone, expression, and gesture as instruments of expression. The writing of dramatic scenes, too, should be attempted and encouraged. History and mythology give splendid material and provide excellent opportunities. It must be apparent that the depiction of certain characters will employ the typical temperament modes. Indeed the four temperaments furnish us with four styles of gesture, bearing, and voice. This offers the teacher an organic and natural way to introduce her class to acting. Needless to say, one does not speak about the temperaments themselves to the children, but uses the typical imagery in one's discussion of one or the other character prior to dramatic action. One could speak somewhat like this, for instance, when speaking to younger students: "Walk like a king; like a warrior; like a very sad man; walk like a good-for-nothing!" Of course one can speak about the fiery, the watery, airy or earthy manner of posture, gesture or gait, as long as one refrains from using terminology like *sanguine*.

> *In a poem everything depends on the way the poet uses the musical element, rhythm, melody, the theme, the imaginative element, the evocation of sound. Single words give the prose content. The crux is how we treat that prose content.*[68]

Speech Sounds and Temperaments

> *He who is not engaged with speech, hearing inwardly—to him come no pictures and no thoughts. He remains clumsy in this thinking, and abstract, if not pedantic, in his speaking. It is just by experiencing the nature of the sounds, the pictorial element in the forming of speech itself, that something lies which conjures out of our souls even the very thoughts we require to present to our audience. In the experiencing of the word lies something creative in relation to our inner being which should never be overlooked. This is extraordinarily important. We ought actually to be ruled by the feeling for how the word, the sequence of words, the formation of words and the formation of sentences are connected with our whole organization. Just as we can solve, in a certain way, the riddle of man from his physiognomy, so can we feel even more what the whole person is like from the way in which he speaks, —not what he says, but how he says it.*[69]

In his *Speech and Drama*, Steiner gives a diagram of the consonant sounds as they correspond to the elements:[70]

Earth	Water	Air	Fire
D			H
T			CH
B			Y
P	L	R	SH
G			S
K			TH
M			F
N			W, V

He indicates further that the earth sounds are related to the visual, the fire sounds to tonal qualities. Why the majority of consonants should be relegated to the earthy and the fiery elements could be an interesting question to ponder.

Language is intimately interwoven with the self—indeed it is the working of the spirit-self into the eternal ego substance. We may see the past self working in the earth sounds and the future self in the fire sounds; we may see the melancholic ego in childhood and the choleric ego in the adult manifested here. The air and water sounds—*R* and *L*—are the mediators and provide the connection between these two, as befits their mercurial mission.

And what is the place of the vowel sounds? The vowel sounds are, as it were, the bridge from within an individual to the without, from the without to the within; they are the bridge between individual and world.

The breath stream differentiates from within outwards—from the feeling of unity to the confrontation with diversity. The vowels arise at different points along this out-streaming breath. Steiner also refers to the *A* as the feeling element most connected to the inward experience, to the self; the *U* as the one sound going most towards a consonantal experience of the world; and the *I* as standing in between inner emotion and outer form. Thus the *A* sound also carries with it the strongest feeling of unity, the *U* sound the greatest feeling of separation, spoken subjectively, or differentiation, spoken objectively.

The vowel sounds as such are related to the soul realm and thus are present in the middle between the *R* and the *L*. We have here actually a kind of cross of consonants and vowels. It would be an absorbing subject of research to study, if the first sounds pronounced by infants already herald their future temperament type. In a most wonderful way this sequence is related to the incarnating ego, for from the mercurial middle realm, from the widths of the circumference, many a child babbles the *relationship* sounds, then follows the incarnation stream further downwards towards the earth with the crystalline/salty earth consonants which make visible the natural world, and finally lets speech rise up to heaven as a fiery flame.

> *When they speak together, children can do things which they otherwise cannot do, just as a crowd in the street is carried away. The younger the children are, the more deceptive it can become. It is good to pick children out at random to do the same thing on their own. The others then have to be attentive while the chosen one is saying his piece.*[71]

Speaking Temperament Language—a Task for Teachers

Moreover, it is highly important that teachers also work at developing their own speech—musicality, rhythm, clarity, enunciation, plastic force, and so on. If we pay too little attention to our own speech, we cannot create the right medium for communication, we cannot establish the soul mood, which is the basis for our words. (We must remember here the fact that in Waldorf schools the subject matter is at first communicated verbally by the teacher and that textbooks will be used in the higher grades, and then not necessarily to introduce subjects, but rather to practice capacities.) Through the very way we form sounds, words, and sentences, induce tone and coloration, and with it musicality, we permeate our speech and language and thus transmit more than the actual meaning of the words. We *clothe* the words, for used only abstractly they would remain *naked*. It is in this very realm that temperament quality lives in language and speech, and that teachers may learn to speak *temperament language.*

This is one huge area of interest which we cannot include in these pages: That is the typical and characteristic coloration of different languages through the usage of sound that relates to the respective temperaments. This area would also be fertile ground for future research.

If we infuse ourselves with the qualities of air, our very speech will reflect this airiness; if we unite ourselves with water, our very speech will become watery. If we allow earth and fire to play in too, then our speech will reflect these modes also. This is the way to introduce temperament qualities into our own speech.

A kind of reverse process holds good for teacher than for student: We have first to make alive within us the image and then our bodily expression in gesture and speech sounds will follow. Even our feeling—intangibly interwoven with our very words—will ring deeply and stream out towards our students. Of course, to begin with, it is essential also to practice the deliberate use of certain sounds and sound sequences until we develop instinctively the right feeling for them. This practice enables us also to achieve greater clarity of diction.

Indeed, as pointed out above, we cannot begin to do our work as teachers without infusing our feeling for the qualities of sounds into the way we speak. If we feel ourselves empathetically into the very sounds of words, if we develop a *sound image* of each word, then we may deepen our understanding, and eventually our concepts and images will take on a living quality. Thus we awaken in ourselves sensitivity for qualitative sound values.

Truly, in working with the musicality of language, with its structure and its sounds, we are at work in a wonderfully heavenly interval: a divine pause, a spiritual hiatus between our future and the student's past. We entice the student from his or her givens from the past, which has shaped the gifts, into this divine hiatus. The immediate present may enter in the guise of language, the form of the word, and work creatively at shaping the student's future. Here an intangible equilibrium is created which bears within it the potential of communication from soul to soul, from individual to individual, from one generation to another.

> *That which we have as the art of pedagogy will have its physical form only in our next incarnation. Every trait in us which is worthy to be imitated, or which is the foundation for our authority, is present in us germinally and will form our next incarnation. Our own future incarnation—when we are active as educators—holds a dialogue with the past incarnations of our students.*[72]

So we have with the melancholic earth sounds that which is most clearly created by the past. The fire sounds stream cholerically in the impulses and beings looking in from the future. The soul sounds proper, the vowels flanked by *L* and *R*, provide the possibilities that these two sound families—past and future—may meet, and commune with each other, and thus flow and stream and bring word into being.

> *Read a fairy tale, pointing and delicately chiseling the consonants, and you will have the impression, not indeed of something natural, but of something that is gently suggestive of the eerie, the ghostly. And this is how it should be with a fairy tale. The vowel intonation being allowed to subside, the vowels slip away into consonants, and as a result the whole thing is lifted a little out of reality. We are no longer in immediate reality. We receive the impression of something a little uncanny. The fairy tale, you see, treats what belongs to the sense world as if it were supersensible, and only when it is told or read in the way I have described can our human feeling be reconciled to it.*[73]

Consonants describe the tangible existence of the world around us—the finished creation in the earth sounds, the potential creation in the fire sounds. Vowels carry the soul mood. By learning to use sounds appropriately we may paint a living soul mood for our listeners.

To return to style: We may relate the contemplative/descriptive epic style to the ample use of the earth sounds. Further we may relate dramatic writing to the use of the fire sounds. And we may use the vowels in combination with air and water sounds best in developing a lyrical style and mood.

From fourth grade on we may discuss the suitability of certain words for specific purposes with the students. Learning about appropriate word usage, now from an artistic viewpoint, is an important aspect of language arts. In making a comparison between the sound picture of a word and its meaning, we do much to develop in children a sensitivity towards the musicality of language.

The temperament modalities act out their being in each word, in each sentence, and also in each piece of writing. Through them we may catch a glimpse of the living weaving of the essential character of different languages, as they sound through the centuries, as they inspire us, and thus also make our students aware of the wondrous process by which human beings recreate themselves in language.

PART THREE

Chapter Eight

Temperaments and the Fourfold Organization of the Human Being

As long as we cannot pursue the activities of the different states of matter, water, air and fire in particular organs, the soul nature will also not reveal itself to us. At first we must condense the soul nature, then we arrive at man's physical nature. But in penetrating through the latter we arrive at the soul-spiritual foundations of our physical organization.[74]
— Rudolf Steiner

The above quotation imparts to us the key which our own cognition must use if we hope to come to an understanding of the human soul: We need to learn to follow the different states of matter—earth, water, air and fire—as they work within the human being. Then we shall be able to penetrate to the spiritual foundation of our physical organization. These different states of matter are the tools by which we may recognize the pathways of the human soul and spirit essence, as they work into the bodily organization. For, as Rudolf Steiner points out repeatedly, it is very essential to remember that in this our time, which has lost the instinctive knowledge of these matters, the spiritual forces need a foothold in the physical world before they are able to manifest and work therein. We have attempted to indicate that this foothold exists in the working of the elemental/etheric forces, which form a ladder, as it were, between the heavenly forces (or energies) and beings, which descend into the world of physical forces and material substance, and thus work actively into it.

The Elements and Human Physiology

Behold the earthy human—the mineral skeleton—solid, dense, heavy and contracted. We see the physical body carried by the mineralized skeleton. It is the hardest part of the body and subject to the physical laws of gravity, the carrier of weight, of measure, mathematically proportioned regarding the size of bones. The skeleton is actually, though apparently the lowest of members, the creation of high spiritual beings, the Spirits of Form. Steiner describes it thus: *The bony system is the Man of Imagination filled out with matter.*[75]

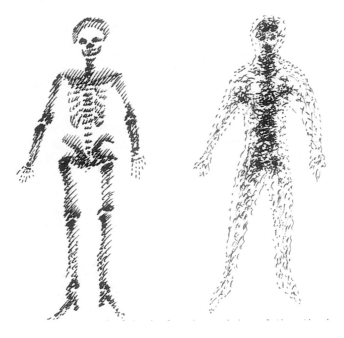

The watery human is all fluid motion, is constantly waxing and waning, secreting, dissolving and coagulating. This is the alchemist of the body, who manifests through the vortices of the glands, which are retorts and alembics. The watery human is the physical basis for the activity of the etheric body: It represents rhythmically flowing interchanges, the sensitive modulations of the time body as our inner water organization swells and diminishes, often following moon and tides.

Seeing the watery human and the earthy human together, we may behold the caduceus of the major blood vessels, as it were, winding around the fluid contained in the spinal column and the brain—this indicates the healer in us, our own etheric body. Musical rhythm reveals the etheric in human beings. Steiner describes this in his lectures on *Eurythmy as Visible Music* (Rudolf Steiner Press, London, 1977, GA 278, Lecture of February 22, 1924): *It is the etheric in man which is revealed in rhythm.*

The glands secrete in cyclical rhythms. The sap of our body rises and sinks, and our own inner seasons of the year are carried out simultaneously and contracted, as it were, instead of being spread out over time.

> *The spiritual insight into human nature will show us that in the first moments of sleep spring-life sprouts and blossoms in us, and when we awaken autumn sinks into us like the setting sun.*[76]

The formative forces in their elemental polarity—expanding, contracting, sinking, rising, giving way to gravity, resurrecting into levity (as the opposite of gravity), as they flow and float—perform a musical symphony of intricate timing in that liquid mother lode of the etheric body, in the mercurial fluid organization of each human body, which carries this nexus of life forces.

The airy human has a very curious shape. It is centered in organs around the larynx. The cavities of the skull—sinuses and Eustachian tubes, pharynx, larynx, and esophagus—reach down into the lungs which branch out in delicate and minuscule alveoli; these are all part of the form of airy human. The outgoing breath also belongs to the human air organization. Especially in speaking, this breath is modulated and formed in currents, eddies, and vibrations and is thereby part of the air organization.

The human astral body has its basis in the physical element of air—a very volatile basis, as the actual air changes through the carbon-oxygen metabolism. The stable element in the air is the nitrogen, which has been called by Steiner the carrier of the astral principle.

> *Everywhere—in the animal kingdom and in the plant and even in the Earth—the bridge between carbon and oxygen is built by nitrogen. And the spirituality which—once again with the help of sulphur—is working thus in nitrogen, is that which we are wont to describe as the astral. It is the*

astral spirituality in the human astral body. It is the astral spirituality in the Earth's environment. For as you know, there too the astral is working—in the life of plants and animals, and so on.[77]

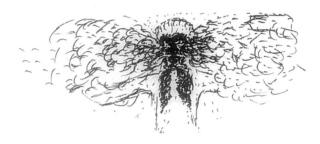

And finally fire—the warmth human within us. The internal organs such as the heart, liver, spleen and stomach, are the greatest concentration of inner heat—they are our inner furnaces. Along the thin threads of the arteries heat travels to the extremities, but around our limbs—particularly hands and feet—there are potentially large areas of heat, which manifest as soon as we are engaged in physical activity and work. We have actually a twofold fire nature—an internal and an external warmth organization. For even as we walk over the ground, we leave not only the marks of our foot steps, but we also leave a slight temperature trace. We leave it in the air as we work or play, so that there is actually a cloud of heat continuously trailing us.

Fire is the physical foothold of the ego. The ego follows the warmth of the blood in its circulation. The ego of man is twofold: an outer ego and also an inner ego active in man.

Steiner, in *Education for Special Needs* [78] develops the picture of the twofold working of the ego by using a diagram in the form of a *lemniscate* to illustrate, in this abbreviated notation, how the four principles of the human being work into each other. The twofold signature of the ego, as expressed diagrammatically in a lemniscate, is thus mirrored by the human warmth organization, revealing an outer and an inner region of human activity. The fourfold human organization is integrated and united because the four elements, as they work within each individual—which is not identical to their working in nature, but correlative—anchor down each constitutional part within the physical.

It is thus the activity of the elements that integrates the human spirit within the body. The temperaments, which are the time signatures of the elements as they express themselves in the peculiarities of the formative processes, may be seen therefore as the integrating agents linking the eternal human entity to its temporal part in the course of the incarnation process. For the teacher, Steiner's elaborations of the workings of the elements in human beings are therefore of immense significance.

> *But if the bodily substance is traced back to warmth, a bridge can be built from what exists in the body as warmth to what works from out of the soul into the warmth in the human organism. There is warmth both without and within the human organism. As we have heard, in man's constitution warmth is an organism; the soul, the soul-and-spirit, takes hold of this warmth-organism and by way of the warmth all that becomes active which we inwardly experience as the moral.* [79]

The element of warmth is therefore the driving force of the incarnation process.

At this point in our deliberations it should become increasingly apparent that we aid the incarnation process of a child considerably when using the time and form language of the temperaments in our classroom practice.

The Shift of Temperament from Childhood to Adulthood

In the fifth lecture of *Discussions with Teachers* (Rudolf Steiner Press, London, 1983), Steiner points out the following relationship between the four constituent principles of the human being and the temperaments:

Ego	Melancholic
Astral	Choleric
Etheric	Sanguine
Physical	Phlegmatic

If there is a slight predominance of one principle over the others, it results in a characteristic temperament picture. As the being of the child incarnates, and favors, as it were, a slightly stronger bond with one of its constituent principles, the temperament picture comes about.

But as the child grows up, its temperament will change. Steiner indicates this change in the lecture mentioned above in the following way:

The	melancholic	will tend to become a	choleric.
The	choleric	will tend to become a	sanguine.
The	sanguine	will tend to become a	phlegmatic.
The	phlegmatic	will tend to become a	melancholic.

In the adult, the predominance of the ego over the other members is expressed through a choleric tendency, the predominance of the astrality through a sanguine tendency, the predominance of the etheric through a phlegmatic, and the predominance of the physical through a melancholic inclination. It needs to be mentioned yet again, that with most individuals the temperament tendencies and inclinations are subtle. It is an unusual person who shows a strong and obvious temperament picture in his or her behavior.

How are we to understand this shift between childhood and adult temperament? It can only be understood by following the inner dynamics of the incarnation process. I offer here one approach to this problem.

Taking several successive incarnations of an individual, we may form a picture of transformation from the body of the one incarnation into the head of the following one. Here we should visualize, as literally and concretely as our imagination allows, Steiner's repeated descriptions.

Then we may combine the above picture with Steiner's descriptions and our own observations of the formative processes in the first nine years of life. Thus we might come to the conclusion that these formative processes begin in the previous incarnation, are then continued by the human soul with the help of the angelic, hierarchical beings of the cosmos, and come to a certain conclusion around the ninth year of life.

A further dimension of this formative process is added by considering the activity of the soul forces: the cognitive capacities of perception and thinking, the emotional capacities of the feeling life, and the volitional capacities, particularly directed intentionality. Their activity can be regarded as being instrumental in transforming the seeds of one incarnation into the fruits of the next. Thinking links the individual with the residue of the past, volition prepares seeds for the future, whereas feeling/emotion balances both in the present.[80]

Steiner also uses the diagram of an involuting and exvoluting spiral when describing the incarnation process:

The past comes over, penetrates into and is enveloped by our present spirit, out of whom radiates our life of soul—our thinking, feeling and willing. Thinking as it were secretes to one side the physical body, to the other the etheric body; feeling secretes to one side the etheric body, to the other the astral body; willing to one side the astral body, to the other the ego. Thus we may say: All this develops germinally into the future, in order to form new realms.[81]

Here we have the cause underlying the twofold working of the ego: We have in one incarnation the formative and contracting forces of the ego working into our physical organization as exemplified by the human head organization and the capacity and power of thinking; we also have the activity of the body—as directed by human intentionality—as the seed for our future incarnation. Indeed, one may say that in any one incarnation we do not have a complete ego.

> Yet it is really no more than the semblance of the I [ego] that falls within the field of Earth consciousness; the true I can be seen only by looking back into an earlier incarnation. The I that we have now is in process of becoming; not until our next incarnation will it be a reality.[82]

The contracting process thus continues on long after birth. The formative forces, as we know from Steiner's numerous indications, conclude their main work on the physical body with the formation and eruption of the second teeth, and from then on become available in the realm of the soul for the development and consolidation of the cognitive capacities of memory and thinking.

Thus our *head ego* comes to a certain completion around the ninth year. Its beginning was in the previous incarnation. At which age did a beginning take place?

Around puberty something fundamentally new begins in each individual. Our actions—the result of the working of our *limb ego*—begin to be inscribed into our astral heart, so that they become part of the *burden of karma*. They become seeds for the future. As Steiner expresses in his lecture on *The Human Heart* (*The Human Soul in Relation to World Evolution*, op. cit.), *into this undifferentiated entity* [the astral heart] *all that we do now is inscribed—the movements of our arms and legs, and not only these, but all that we accomplish through our arms and legs.* Our present head-ego had its beginning around puberty in our last incarnation.

To return to the temperaments: If we have a particularly strong affinity for the ego-body, if we have, as it were, entered through its gate into this life, then we shall be strongly related in childhood to the formative forces of the head, which are active out of our own past ego activity in a former life, and so we become a melancholic child. In adulthood we shall then switch over to the strong will forces preparing for our future ego and so become a choleric adult.

If our astral forces are predominant in childhood, we shall be all movement, all activity, sensitivity and awareness, and rush around with choleric liveliness. As an adult we shall have calmed somewhat this dramatic display of activity into the more delicate fluttering about of our feelings and emotions. They now do the moving about instead of our physical limbs. Thus we shall be toned down and become a sanguine adult after having been a choleric child. As a child our consciousness—the astral configuration is also the nexus of consciousness —is in outer movement and the external world; in the adult it rather enters via sensory perception.

If our etheric/formative/life forces are predominant, we feel ourselves related strongly to the whole width of the universe.

> *This is of great significance. On our descent into the earthly world, when we draw to ourselves the forces of the universal ether, we actually take with us in our etheric body a kind of image of the cosmos. If we could extract the etheric body of a man at the moment when he is uniting with the physical, we should have a sphere—far more beautiful than has ever been wrought by mechanical means—a sphere complete with Stars and Zodiac and Sun and Moon.*[83]

This being of tender beauty and rhythmically musical timing expresses itself in the joyful sanguinity of childhood. But as an adult, we shall have arrived on earth, at the real water level of our watery human, having left behind—one level higher—the freedom of the airy nature, and thus will have become a phlegmatic.

If we have a strongly developed physical body, we shall not yet have touched the ground with our feet as a child but remain more connected to the less dense water element of the water sphere, just as we were in the womb. Even our very bones are not yet as hard as they become later on—cartilage substance is less mineralized and solid and is still plastically suffused with liquid. We are less of a mineral human at birth, and through infancy, than after puberty. But the physical hardens and contracts eventually—fluids may solidify—and the phlegmatic child becomes a melancholic adult.

The Human Fourfold Organism and the Life of Soul

To recapitulate: Thinking as a cosmic force extrudes the physical body on the one side, the etheric on the other; feeling as a cosmic force the etheric body on one side, the astral on the other; willing as a cosmic force the astral on one side, and the ego on the other. It is apparent that the actual innermost life of an individual takes place between the etheric and the astral organization, or, to put it another way, in the realm of pure and cosmic empathy and feeling.

It is essential to recognize that a human being's essence is affected by and works into external events on both sides.

> *The body as a whole, not merely the nervous activity impounded in it, is the physical basis of psychic life. And, just as, for ordinary consciousness, psychic life is naturally classifiable in terms of ideation, feeling and willing, so is physical life classifiable in terms of neural function, rhythmic occurrence and metabolic process.*
>
> *The question at once arises: In what way do the following enter and inhabit the organism: on the one hand, sense perception proper, in which neural function merely terminates, and on the other the faculty of motion, which is the effusion of the will?*[84]

This statement is of the utmost importance if we hope to come to some understanding of an individual's relationship to her or his inner soul life, the objective external world and the objective spiritual world. Further, this statement helps us to understand just how the twofold activity of the ego manifests itself.

Steiner uses yet another description of the interrelationship of the forces of the soul and the fourfold human organization. It is an important description because it gives us another key to relate both the threefoldness of cognitive, emotional and volitional capacities, with their adjuncts of sense-perception on one side and the ability for motion on the other, and the fourfoldness of the physical, the etheric, the astral and the ego organization as expressed in the different parts of human physiology.

Head: The ego, astral body and etheric are free from organic activity to some extent; therefore they are able to work together into the thinking process.

Chest and Trunk: The etheric body slips into the glands. They do not like it and secrete immediately. The etheric body also slips into the muscles, which do not protest. Feeling takes place in the free remaining part of the astral and ego body.

Limbs and Metabolism: The etheric body enters deeply into organic processes. During the day—the time of waking consciousness—the astral organization accompanies the etheric into a deep involvement with organic processes. The individual only experiences the ego, the essence of the self, with his or her awareness, and intentionality comes about.

Thinking, as it were, requires least the support of the physical and of its organic processes, feeling a little more so, and our intentionality in the will still more so.[85] The three states of human consciousness are bound up with the interrelationship and interaction between the parts of the fourfold organization. We are fully awake in the region of our head, we are a-dream in the region of our rhythmical processes, and we are asleep in the area of our will and metabolic processes.

Let us realize that we are most awake in that area of our physical body where the physical forces are left to themselves most by our higher members; we are a-dream where the etheric suffuses the physical body organically; we are asleep where the astral body is also immersed in the physical organic processes.

The transition point of the free and the partially bound etheric activity is at the larynx, situated at the crossing point between head and body. It is there that concept is bound to the word, through the interaction between the etheric and the astral forces of a human being. Let us remember here again Steiner's diagram of the lemniscate in his *Education for Special Needs*, as mentioned above, which shows the interaction of the four members.

The Temperaments as Filters between Cosmos and Individual

Temperaments are agents of transformation. As such they are active at the border regions between body and soul life. They are, as it were, filters between cosmos and individual. In sense-perception,

> [t]he external world reaches out into the senses, as though they were bays or inlets leading into the organism's own existence. Compassing the processes that take place in the senses, the psyche does not participate in inner organic events; it participates in the extension of outer events into the organism.[86]

It is here that one of the filtering activities of the temperament processes occurs. On the borderline, where the external facts impinge upon the etheric body through our sense perception, the temperament mode puts its particular coloring in between, and we experience the world filtered and colored by our own temperament because we look through it into the world, as through a pair of colored glasses. Thus everything around us that is similar to our own temperament mode will be more noticeable to us than anything that is different in temperament mode. The fiery in the world will be particularly impressive to the choleric, the airy to the sanguine, and so forth.

Conversely, whenever we act out of our own soul activity in order to impress ourselves upon this outer world, likewise we have to cross a borderline.

> In the same way, when physical motion is brought about, what we have to do with is not something that is actually situated within the organism, but an outward working of the organism into the physical equilibrium (or other dynamic relation) between the organism itself and its environment. Within the organism it is only a metabolic process

that can be assigned to willing; but the event that is liber-
ated through this process is at the same time an actual hap-
pening within the equilibrium, or the dynamics, of the ex-
ternal world. Exerting volition the life of the psyche over-
reaches the domain of the organism and combines its action
with a happening in the outer world.[87]

On this border, on the portal from which we launch the impulses
of our inner soul life into external reality by originating activity and motion, the intentions of our soul life pass the zone of the temperaments and
thus our action, our motion, is filtered and formed in a typical way, corresponding to our particular temperament mode.

It has now become apparent just where we must search for the
realm of the activity of the temperaments in relation to our soul life—it is
the region where soul and body, self and cosmos meet each other. Temperaments thus appear as the modifiers of the internalization process of
our sense perception as well as of the externalization process by which
directed volition and intentionality express themselves in movement, and
potentially creative activity. Language may show one of the most intimate
expressions of soul life in the area of language which is not connected
with abstract meaning—the emotional and musical sound formation,
which colors the pictorial quality of words.

Temperaments express the time body of an individual—they
modify her or his impressions, expressions, and therefore also language,
in the typical imagery derived from the elements of nature. They are the
elements of nature drawn into the realm of the individual, and thus individualized to a certain extent, in such a way that we have in the temperaments a zone in each human being which belongs to outer nature and to
inner soul configuration at one and the same time. In the temperament
zone, individual human and cosmos overlap.

Temperament stands in the middle between what we bring with us
as individuals and what originates from the line of heredity. When
the two streams unite, the one stream colors the other. They color
each other reciprocally. Just as blue and yellow, let us say, unite in
green, so do the two streams in man unite in what we call tempera-
ment. What mediates between all inner characteristics that he brings
with him from his earlier incarnation on the one side, and on the

other what the line of heredity brings to him, comes under the con-
cept temperament. It now takes its place between the inherited char-
acteristics and what he has absorbed into his inner essential being.[88]

The tempera-
ments thus emerge as me-
diators, which link person
with person, individual
with world, and each
person's own eternal and
temporal being. In order to
teach, in order to commu-
nicate, we must learn to
speak the language of the
temperaments.

Chapter Nine

Temperament Characteristics in Relation to Formative and Movement Forces in the Human Being

The movement forces are the forces underlying all possibilities of free movement—in human being and animal—and originate not in the earthly realm but in the cosmos, particularly in the planetary spheres. The concept of movement should be taken in its widest sense—namely, to include all movement surging through our being, in body as well as in soul and spirit. Thus bodily motion, soulful emotion and varying degrees and states of consciousness are linked up with the working of the planetary forces upon human beings. Because of their planetary origin, Rudolf Steiner also refers to them as astral forces.

The formative forces of the etheric world are the agents of all the life processes in human beings. They also are the archetypal forces working in the temperament characteristics of each individual. We know that we have no direct control over the life processes in us, though we may be able to influence them via living habits, food and medicine. But direct control, by and large, eludes us at this stage of our development.

The movement-consciousness forces, on the other hand, are to a certain extent under our conscious control. We are aware of being involved in specific movements. We may have quite specific feelings, thoughts, reactions, and intentions regarding our movements, even if we do not understand quite how they come about. We are at least able, with our consciousness, to observe our bodily movements while we execute them. We are also partially aware—though we cannot control them as well—of the emotions acting on the stage of our soul. Thus there is a very definite link between movement and consciousness.

Form comes about as the result of movement. It is the residue, the memory of a process, of something that has been in motion at an earlier time. Movement implies a change in size, location, dimension, form, organization, color and sound, in particular direction, in evolving and devolving sequence, repeatedly or uniquely. These two principles—

form and movement—are in constant interaction throughout human life and permeate every aspect and experience.

The etheric forces as the agents of the formative processes of life are themselves in constant movement and change. We must try to understand the duality of the formative and the movement forces to understand the human temperaments.

The Polarizing Powers

Steiner describes, in *The World of the Senses and the World of the Spirit* (op. cit.), one aspect of the disarray brought about in the inner organization of human beings by the luciferic influence. This particular description is vital to our present considerations:

> It is obvious that the first disarrangement to come about was what we have called the preponderance of the I over the astral body. All the Luciferic power was given to the I and the I got impurely mixed up with thinking, feeling and willing, and then maintained the Luciferic preponderance over the astral body. The astral body in consequence was able to gain ascendancy on its part over the etheric body. And thus the whole balance in man was upset. It is just as though by the Luciferic influence a blow had been dealt at the astral body, and the astral body had passed it on and so gained an ascendancy over the etheric. But it can go no further that way. The etheric body does not hand on the blow. It is like hitting a rubber ball. You can push into the ball for a certain distance but then it comes back again. So we can speak of a preponderance of astral over etheric body that rebounds and asserts predominance over the astral, giving us a reverse predominance of what we had before. And then follows the predominance of physical body over the etheric body. These latter two strike in the opposite direction. Why do they strike back? It comes about because while here Lucifer is striking in, Ahriman, in the physical and etheric body, is striking back from the other side. Here in the middle, where you have on the one hand the ascendancy of etheric body over astral body and physical body over the etheric body, and on the other hand the ascendancy of astral body over etheric

154

body and I over astral body—here in the middle you have
Lucifer and Ahriman in collision. Here they come up against
one another. Thus, there is in man a center point where
Lucifer and Ahriman meet in their own true nature. And
man can either swing in the direction of Lucifer and bore
his astral body deeper than is right into his etheric body, or
he can take hold of the impetus in the power of Ahriman
and strike the etheric body too deep into the astral body.
Such are the dynamic effects with which we have to deal.[89]

The implications of the above passage are far-reaching. Not only do we have to consider the interactions of forces within our inner organization but also the workings of spiritual beings—Lucifer and Ahriman—who ever attempt to use these forces to their own ends. To ignore the working of these beings would result in a superficial treatment of our topic.

Steiner describes at length the working of two spiritual beings, who, though vastly more powerful than human beings, have lagged behind in their own evolution. Lucifer and Ahriman thus belong to a group of cosmic beings not in step with the forward evolution of humanity and cosmos as directed by hierarchical beings of many ranks. Because they are out of step in many respects, they act as spirits of hindrance and are allowed to function so that individual human beings may wake up when facing and overcoming the obstacles they create. Lucifer's influence is felt more within the human soul. He attempts to hold individuals back by promising them paradisiacal states of innocence and delight. Ahriman drives an individual more deeply into materialism. He attempts to convince one that she or he—a human being—has no spiritual, nor even an independent, soul nature; that the inner life consists only of animal instincts. He aims to rob individuals totally of their divinity and enslave them through their bodies. Opponents, Lucifer and Ahriman cooperate with each other so that their shared goal, to tear human beings apart, may eventually come about. Unknown to our ordinary consciousness, there is a bitter struggle going on in our inner being between the formative and the transformative forces, as the movement forces may also be called.

If we picture again the four qualities of the four elements as we have done it in Chapter 1, we may state that the earthy and the watery elements show more a fixing of form, whereas the airy and fiery states of matter display a tendency to dissolve form. Thus the former tend towards a formative, the latter towards a more transformative activity.

It is good to picture as vividly as possible the tendency towards densification and fixation of the one pole and the tendency towards dissolution and transformation of the other. We could also use the terms contraction and expansion to describe this polarity. The earthy element is the one suffering the greatest contraction, whereas the watery element is already far less subjected to this. Air is taken hold of by the expanding forces, and fire is itself an active agent of expansion.

The two spiritual beings mentioned here—Lucifer and Ahriman—who are actively engaged in a struggle for preponderance in the inner being of individuals, are related to this polarity. Lucifer works in the expansive principle, thus the elements of fire and air are *his* elements. Therefore, the choleric and the sanguine temperaments are, as it were, his temperaments also. Ahriman works primarily with contraction, thus the earthy element is particularly permeated by his activity.[90]

The watery element—the element most purely representing the ever flowing, weaving, undulating, fluctuating, etheric forces, may be taken as manifesting a dynamic equilibrium between the polarity of contraction and expansion.

> So one can say that the soul-life opens out and then draws itself together, expands and contracts—only as we say this we must not let any space conceptions mix in with it. During this expansion and contraction one thing is unquestionably present, and that is inner spiritual movement. MOVEMENT! Soul-life is movement. Only we must think of movement not as movement in space but as we have described it. And this expansion and contraction gives forms. So you have movement, and the outer expression of movement in certain forms. The forms here meant are not spatial forms, but forms of expanding and contracting soul-life. And what lives in this expansion and contraction? You will get near the reality if you consider a little what must live therein. Therein live your feelings, thoughts, impulses of will, insofar as that is all spiritual.[91]

It is obvious from the above two quotations that the terms *expansive* and *contractive* are to be taken in a qualitative, not a quantitative/spatial context.

Here we are still groping at the simplest possible picture in our attempt to lead into the complexities of the human being. In order to proceed, we must also take into consideration the relationship of psychological and physiological processes, as hinted at already several times, for a human being is a whole, albeit a very complex whole.

The Working of the Polarizing Powers within Human Physiology

If we examine the consequences of expansive and contractive activities in terms of physiological processes, we find that the glandular secretions hold a middle position, though we might assume that actual secretion would be related to a form of contraction.

Sensory perception, on the other hand, is definitely a form of contraction. In focusing on a facet of our surrounding world we contract our consciousness, as it were, to a point, and direct it outwards to the object of our perception. We individualize and separate our sense perceptions from each other when we concentrate on one. No wonder that melancholics not only usually have an excellent gift of observation, but that sense perceptions make a particularly strong and lasting imprint on them.

The phlegmatic delights more, possibly, at the stimulation of his glandular processes, including the flow of his digestive juices. On the other hand, when the expanding processes are active we have a preponderance of the astral over the etheric forces. Steiner links them also with the digestive processes. The purpose of these digestive processes is the integration of external forces and the transformation of external substance. Assimilation and unification come about.

The breathing process presents a more tentative unification with the external world than the digestive process. With every exhalation we separate ourselves from the surrounding air, with every inhalation we unite ourselves with it. Within our body, we unite oxygen with the blood and separate out carbon dioxide. This rhythmical exchange in the realm of the air—also a metabolic process—is probably most related to the sanguine temperament in terms of man's physiological configuration.

The processes of nutrition require still greater energy than the breathing processes. Our digestive organs develop much internal heat.

There is, indeed, a veritable internal furnace at work in our digestion, through which we unite certain forces with our organization. This unification, though, occurs only after a complex, detailed and intense destruction process of the actual nutrients.

Choleric and sanguine people find it easier to identify with others, thus expanding their awareness to include others as part of their environment. Expansion also fosters unification. Our blood is the physiological agent of unification, as it courses through the body binding its organs together, just as the nervous system is the physiological agent of diversification. The choleric has a strong affinity with the workings of the blood circulation, as he or she works with the constructive and destructive forces of the digestion that permeate, transform, assimilate and humanize external substances and forces. The melancholic is orientated towards the sensory-nerve process, focusing, contracting and separating from the world. The sanguine, and to a still greater degree, the phlegmatic, oscillate more or less harmoniously between contraction and expansion, diversification and unification, blood processes and nerve processes.

We have suggested several connecting links between a person's psychological and physiological essence. Let us not forget that the interaction of the ahrimanic and the luciferic entities, working into each person, involve directly the activity of the temperaments, the elements and the etheric forces. The fourfold qualities of the temperaments provide the connecting bridge between the polarities, which we have attempted to characterize in simple form.

Aspects of Upper and Lower Human Physiology

The Earth's surface is a real organ, which—if you will— you may compare to the human diaphragm. . . . In the individuality with which we are here concerned, the head is beneath the surface of the Earth, while we, with all the animals, are living in the creature's belly! Consider, once more, that entire element in the neighborhood of the Earth in which we ourselves are living and breathing and from which the plants, along with us, receive their outer warmth and air, and even water. All this actually corresponds to that which would represent, in man, the abdominal organs. On the other hand, that which takes place in the inte-

*rior of the Earth—beneath the Earth's surface—works upon
the plant-growth in the same way in which our head works
upon the rest of our organism, notable in childhood, but
also throughout our life. There is a constant and living
mutual interplay of the above-the-earth and the below-the-
earth.*[92]

The above passage adds yet another polarity to be considered.
These cosmic forces may be described further. Steiner refers here to the
forces in the surrounding atmosphere, above the ground, as the forces
working into the earth sphere from the planetary spheres of Moon, Mercury and Venus as they modify the Sun influence. The forces working
more deeply into the earth, under the surface, stem from Mars, Jupiter
and Saturn, and are then reflected above the ground. How delicate the
interplay is between the telluric and the cosmic polarities is indicated here
by Steiner's following statement:

*The air too is permeated by a delicate vitality the moment it
is absorbed and drawn into the Earth. So it is both with the
warmth and with the air; they take on a slightly living quality when they are received into the Earth. The opposite is
true of the water and of the solid earthy element itself. They
become still more dead inside the Earth than they are outside it. They lose something of their external life. Yet in this
very process they become open to receive the most distant
cosmic forces.*[93]

The forces of warmth and light in cosmos and human being correspond to expanding forces; the water and earth forces to contracting
forces. We are imbedded into a continuous interaction of these forces in
the natural world around us. They enter into us in various ways, are molded
by our own etheric organism, and work in diverse ways in the different
parts of our body. They mediate continuously, as it were, between the
tangible and the intangible, the weighty and the imponderable. In each
individual person they are differentiated in various ways. However, we are
not torn apart by the polarity of these forces.

Accordingly if we accept levity as the representative of all other imponderable forces, we must conceive the whole of external nature as involved in the struggle between levity and gravity, between the force that strives towards the extra-terrestrial and the force that makes earth's substances tend towards the center. We have here the polarity between levity and gravity; and in between that which perpetually seeks the mercurial element is simply something that continually seeks to maintain a state of equilibrium between levity and gravity.[94]

Steiner gives still more detailed descriptions of how the four elements are active in the human body. In the same course of lectures (*Spiritual Science and Medicine)* he speaks of the four meteorological organs and their relation to the elements. He correlates the lungs with the center of the earth processes in the human being, the liver with the water processes, the kidneys with air processes and the heart with warmth processes, thus establishing each of these inner organs as a center of the four elemental forces.

All these four organs work of course into the totality of the human organization. The heart acts as the organ with which an individual's upper body is able to sense the activities of the lower body. It is situated quite near the diaphragm and plays the central role in keeping both parts of man's organic activity apart, but at the same time also linked together. There is a relationship of inversion, as well as correlation between these two polar parts of each person. In nature it is the element of fire which constitutes the bridge between the physical elements and the etheric forces, working imponderably into these physical elements.[95]

The choleric temperament is simply the one that brings the heart function in an individual to the foreground; the phlegmatic element would bring the liver function, the melancholic element the lung function and the sanguine element the kidney function to a slightly more pronounced expression. But as we all need all four inner organs to function for the sake of our well-being, it must be apparent yet again that in each person all four temperaments are active, even if one incarnating soul uses, as it were, one of these organs as its principal gate of entry.

Turning again to another polarity, which we touched upon earlier, the polarity of the working of ahrimanic and luciferic beings into the human psyche, we may consider the following connections. The luciferic beings, working within the human head, would actually prevent human beings from establishing a relationship with the mineral world. They would prefer human beings to be concerned only with the realm of plants and animals. These beings endow us with artistic inclinations and capacities. They belong to the expanding polarity, drawing individuals, if they will allow it, away from the earth.

The other beings, the ahrimanic ones, would like to instill in us a hatred of all past evolution; they would like to exterminate the natural world, even the human world, and create a new evolution of machines.[96] We may recognize in twentieth century science and fantasy fiction many elements of the aspirations of these two groups of entities, as they would entice humanity to forget their human mission in earth evolution.

We must realize, that through being permeated by the formative forces and the elements, humanity participates in the processes of the great world, the cosmos, or as it has been called in earlier ages, the macrocosm. Thus we share in universal life and destiny.

The Bridge between the Polarities

In the on-going interaction between these polar opposite universal powers, between terrestrial and cosmic forces, expanding and contracting forces, luciferic and ahrimanic forces, each human being has become the stage for an equilibration process. One of the most wonderful gifts of angelic beings to humanity, a gift that bears within it an instrument of this equilibration process, is language. Language has its realm in the interplay between the etheric and the astral bodies. Movement forces and formative forces create in their interaction a language person.

> *The artist must have felt—I do not say he must have seen, but he must have experienced in feeling what it means when we say that through the working together of astral body and ether body a second man has been begotten within us, has been set free within us, and lives in speech.*[97]

Small wonder that in the realm of language we take hold of the working of the four elements, the four qualities, the four temperament modalities, most easily and naturally.

A human being stands upright on the surface of the earth. From the distances of the cosmos stream forces, some remaining in the upper body, some entering the earth and working upwards from below. They are caught up, reflected, and echo in each individual repeatedly, thus creating a whole symphony of delicate form and movement. The etheric world fluctuates around him, in color, light and sound, separated from but active within physical matter. An ocean of beings, at work in various ways, surrounds him. Each individual human being is the bridge, and the door through which these forces and beings work upon human nature. Within each person's essential self and organization we may find the heavenly ladder, upon which cosmic forces ascend and descend. It is the ladder of the elements and etheric forces. Each person's ego and astral organization have a foothold in the human body through the warmth and air configuration. The physical and etheric forces work particularly through the earth and water configurations. This is the bridge, the ladder, which enables the human being to be an integrated being of body, soul, and spirit.

We may perceive the elements and the etheric/formative forces as the rungs on the heavenly ladder. If we transform this image a little, we might arrive at the tones of a scale—and perceive the sequence of formative/elemental forces as a heavenly scale, resounding and echoing through an individual. Older world conceptions had still this very picture of a human being's direct relation with this cosmic scale: the harmonies of the spheres. Each planetary orbit was regarded as sounding on one tone, so that the whole solar system sounded together in universal harmony.

Steiner describes the human etheric body as consisting of musical tone: the head part is melody, the chest part is harmony, and the limb part is rhythm. In the head part there is the sequence of tones, in the chest part the simultaneous sounding of tones, and in the limb part of the human etheric body lies hidden the rhythmical configuration uniting the other two parts. Thus the human etheric body is a time body, for rhythm arises within the flow of time. As we mentioned above, the formative forces work in time.[98]

We shall find many times over that musical imagery and musical concepts are necessary for developing an understanding of the temperaments.

Unity, Diversity and Their Equilibrium

The polarity of diversifying and unifying forces, as mentioned already, winds like a red thread through all realms of nature, as well as through human physiological and psychological processes. To reiterate: We may correlate the fiery and airy elements as forming the basis for the unifying principle. The earthy element forms, in its contractive and separating action, the basis for individuation and differentiation processes. The watery element holds the balance. Its mercurial pattern mediates between these two aspects of polarity.

The ahrimanic beings strive to differentiate and individualize to a destructive extreme, the luciferic beings to unify everything they influence. The mercurial beings in the realm of the etheric forces and the temperaments swing in variable rhythmic sequence between these two extremes.

In the realm of the human body, the unifying and converging forces are concentrated in the head, the diverging and individualizing forces in the metabolism and the limb system. The mercurial principle has its seat in the rhythmic/breathing system.

In the realm of the soul, the unifying forces work in thinking, the individualizing forces in the will. However, as will power is also exerted in the activity of thinking, and wish, intention and forethought enter the area of the will, these two areas interpenetrate each other and work together in making up the complexity of our soul life.

> We saw that thinking, as it expresses itself in the superficial soul-life, has behind it a synthesizing activity which operates in the construction and organization of the brain; and then we saw how behind expressions of will is an analytical activity which underlies the organs—underlies indeed our whole metabolism-and-limbs man, keeping the organs separate and distinct one from another.[99]

In the world of nature we rarely find that one single element works in isolation. This is also true in respect of human beings: Rarely do we find just one temperament in excess, without the accompaniment of the others. We need to keep this in mind.

*Thus there is a kind of weaving of life in-between destruc-
tion and solidification of earth existence: luciferic,
ahrimanic. The luciferic element actually tends continuously to make part of man non-material, to lift man away
from earth existence; Lucifer desires, if he but could, to spiri-
tualize, to de-materialize us entirely. But Ahriman is his
opponent; he acts such that all that which Lucifer gouges
out is continually filled in again. Ahriman is the eternal
'concretor.' If you could form Lucifer and Ahriman plastically then you could easily—if matter were interpenetrable—
always push Ahriman into the cavities made by Lucifer, or
cover Lucifer with Ahriman. But, as there are also inner
cavities, one has also to cover them on the inside. Ahriman
and Lucifer, they are the two diametrically opposed powers
active within man. Man himself is the equilibrium. Lucifer's
activity of de-materialization continuously results in
Ahriman's compensating with matter. When we are engaged
in sense perception: that is Lucifer. When we think about
our perceptions: Ahriman. When we decide to form the ideas
of our intentions: Lucifer. When we really direct our will
actively on the earth: Ahriman. Thus man stands between
the two.*[100]

In the above passage, Steiner exemplifies the working together of
the polarities. Let us realize further the extent to which the analytical and
the synthetic tendencies are brought into human beings through the activities of these two cosmic entities. We must realize that we have a synthesizing activity in our perception and an analytical one in thinking. We
have unification, a synthesizing activity in formulating wishes and mo-
tives for future actions, yet an analytical one in our actual intentional
activity.

If we now extend this characteristic picture into the realm of physiology, we have progressive disintegration—the analysis—of the food substance in the digestive process, as it goes from mouth into the digestive
tract. We also have a unifying gesture of the nerves from the periphery of
the body to the spinal chord, and on into the brain.

In our sensory perception we unite with us, via the processes in
the sense organs, something gathered from the external world and inte-

grate it into our memory. In our digestive/metabolic processes we analyze, dissect and separate matter from its form. But we also create our own physical substance through our sensory perceptive processes in what Steiner calls the *cosmic nutrition stream.*[101] At the same time we separate the physical substance of the food we eat from the forces inherent in it, thus discarding the substance and retaining only the forces. This is an analytical process.

Our head synthesizes substance and analyzes forces. One could also speak of world thoughts instead of forces. Conversely, our limb/metabolic configuration synthesizes forces—world thoughts—and analyzes matter. Synthesis and analysis, unity and diversity, contraction and expansion—they all belong to manifestations of the polarity of beings and forces related to the earthy on the one side, and the airy-fiery on the other.

Space, Time, Consciousness:
Their Signature in Temperament Modality

The melancholic, being the person most given up to the contracting polarity, as it works into the mineral realm, will tend to occupy the least extension in space. He will tend to shrink into a point, this being the greatest possible contrast between him and his environment. He will also be very aware of himself as a separate and even isolated person—therefore, the social awkwardness of many melancholics, their feeling of being exposed, their wanting to crawl into the nearest protective space, curl up and give themselves up to thinking, pondering, and reflecting, rather than acting and participating.

He will also try to remain immobile where time is concerned. Thus he will be late, and slow. Time is coming to a rest with him—disrupting and paralyzing the movement of the flow of time—this is the melancholic's natural inclination. To be as immobile as circumstances allow—that is his inclination.

His awareness, too, tends to contract to the smallest possible point—that is, himself. He is, moreover, wide-awake, moreso than a more balanced person. But it is an awareness, an *awakeness*, which is self-centered. His concentration is good but overly attuned to everything that centers on himself—thus making him hypersensitive, at times to the point of hypochondria.

The choleric has a more expansive nature and will tend to take up as much space as she possibly can. She will attempt to unite with her surroundings as fully as possible, thus extending her sphere of activity to bursting point. She treats the whole world as belonging to herself—another facet of an exaggerated unification tendency.

As regards time, she will attempt to overreach herself and therefore tend to be too early, too soon, or too fast. Moreover, she will tend to do more than one thing at a time. Speeding up, accelerating everything she does—this is typical.

Her consciousness is not in her center, but in the circumference. She is not awake and aware through what she senses and thinks as much as through what she does, through her field of action. The choleric, therefore, has her ego experience in her will region more definitively than have the other temperaments. She affirms herself through her actions, thus making it essential for her to be constantly active and on the move. Total involvement at the largest possible scale, grand actions, grand ideas, and grand gestures—this is characteristic of the choleric.

The phlegmatic will also tend to fill out as much space as is available. In contrast, he will not have the same inner urge to go beyond this space as the choleric has, but, rather, like a vessel filling with water, he will—simply—fill it out. He takes all the space he is given not out of an active inner urge but out of inertia. In taking up the space, he will tend to adapt to the given form. Probably the fairest description regarding his feeling for time is this: resting, just slowly moving from action to action, routinely, regularly, and also reliably. Once a movement or activity has begun, inertia will ensure a routinely ongoing continuation. Stopping, however, may again be as difficult as starting had been.

The consciousness of the phlegmatic seems to spread out into the horizontal without a firm and central point of reference. Thus both awareness and *awakeness* of himself, as well as of events around him, are probably at the lowest level compared to the other temperaments, therefore his tendency to sleep through a great deal that jolts others easily awake.

The phlegmatic often develops a highly sophisticated defense mechanism—he will appear to be busy in order to avoid being given more work. He will chatter in order to pretend to be involved with his environment.

The sanguine, on the other hand, will be expansive, though selectively so, in her usage of available space. She will not burst out of the limits, she will wander here and there, able to organize space well and stay within the limits she is given. She will diversify and may be occasionally inconsistent in her usage of space. The quality of her time experience shows itself in her genuine delight in everything that is rhythmical. An even tempo, of course, would be just too boring. But rhythmical change gives great joy to a sanguine's heart. A change of tempo in a recurring rhythm gives her just the right amount of security and challenge at the same time.

Her awareness, too, is definitely directed outward to her environment. Not in the totally involved manner of a choleric, but in the gentler manner of intense curiosity and expectant observation. Also, her intensive craving for sensation and stimulation will cause her difficulties in concentrating on any one object for lengthy periods of time. Indeed, the sanguine has the greatest concentration difficulties, and obstacles in developing staying power, of all the temperaments.

Yet again, we need to point to the fact that no one person represents the exclusive working of any one temperament:

> *A melancholic is only a melancholic because the melancholic temperament predominates in him; for fundamentally everyone is endowed with all four temperaments. Under certain circumstances a melancholic is also phlegmatic, under others he is sanguine and again under others, choleric; the melancholic temperament simply predominates over the other temperaments. And a phlegmatic person is not one who possesses only the phlegmatic temperament, but in whom the phlegmatic temperament is more pronounced, the other temperaments remain in the background.*[102]

Chapter Ten

Bridges of Understanding:
The Real Home of the Temperaments

Thus we are truly, in a certain connection, redeemers of Lucifer. When we begin to be able to love our duty, then the moment has come when we can help towards the redemption and release of the Luciferic powers; we set free the Lucifer forces which are held in us as by a charm, and lead them forth to fight with Ahriman. . . .

Love is the inner fire; its opposite is calmness—the quiet acceptance of what happens in the world. As soon as we approach our right with this quiet and calm interest we call in Ahriman. It is not easy to recognize him here, for we set him free from his merely external existence, we summon him into ourselves and warm him with the love that is already united with right. Calm and peace of mind have the coldness of Ahriman; in the quiet understanding of what is in the world, we unite our warmth and our understanding love with the coldness that is in the outside world. And then we release Ahriman, when we meet what has come about with understanding, when we do not merely demand our rights out of self-love but understand what has come about in the world. This is the eternal battle that is waged between Lucifer and Ahriman.[103]

— Rudolf Steiner

It is only too painfully apparent that we are faced with problems of balance—in our time as well as in our individual lives. In the ever-increasing eccentricity of the swing of the pendulum, which appears to tempt and coerce humanity today towards polarizing every area of human existence, the need to work towards the potential of balance becomes ever greater. We know only too well from Rudolf Steiner's numerous expositions that this balance is not a static and firm point upon which to rest, but an ever-prevailing struggle for equilibrium. An ongoing effort to create balance between the two opposing cosmic powers is demanded from humanity—within physiological and life, psychological, and spiritual processes.

The Quest for Equilibrium

It appears to me that the part of the human organization, which is most exposed to this struggle for balance at the present time, is the etheric body.

A different form of experience will come to the man of modern times. In his own opinion he knows everything so well; he observes the material world, uses his intellect to establish the interconnections between its phenomena and believes that all its riddles are solved in this way, never realizing that he is simply groping in a phantasmagoria. But this way of working coarsens and dries up his ether body, with the ultimate result that the Mephistophelean powers, like a second nature, will attach themselves to him now and in times to come. . . . Nevertheless he will chain a second being to his heels. Accompanied by this second being, he will feel the urge to think materialistic thoughts, to think, not through his own being, but through the second being who is his companion. In an ether body that has been parched by materialism, Mephistopheles will be able to dwell. Understanding what this implies, we shall realize that it is our duty to educate children in the future—be it by way of Eurythmy or the development of a spiritual-scientific outlook—in such a way that they will be competent to understand the spiritual world. The ether body must be quickened in order that the human being may be able to take his rightful stand, fully cognizant of the nature of the being who stands at his side. If he does not understand the nature of this second being, he will be spellbound by him, fettered to him. Just as the Greek was obliged to get the better of the sphinx, so will modern man have to outdo Mephistopheles—with his faunlike, satyr-like form, and his goat's or horse's feet. . . .

The prelude to these happenings is that a people or a poet have premonitions of the existence of the being who accompanies man; but finally, every single human being will have this companion who must not remain unintelligible to him and who will operate most powerfully of all during childhood. If adults whose task it is to educate children today do not know how to deal rightly with what comes to expression in the child, human nature itself will be impaired owing to a lack of understanding of the wiles of Mephistopheles. . . .

I have said already that when etheric forces are impoverished, the feet cannot develop normally, but will wither.[104]

Steiner indicates here in no uncertain terms the actual, yet hidden battle, going on beneath the veils of sense-perceptible existence for each human being's healthy etheric body. Let us try to understand some of the implications of Ahriman's attempt to enter human etheric bodies. Human ether bodies tend to contract, to only fill partially the physical body. Ahriman, as it were, then insinuates himself into the areas of the etheric body which are dried up.

It is a fundamental pedagogical law that one member of human inner organization influences the next lower member—both within each person, as well as in human interaction, such as in the interaction between teacher and student.

If you find that the etheric body of a child is in some way weakened or deficient, you must form, you must modify, your own astral body in such a way that it can work upon the etheric body of the child, correcting and amending it.[105]

It is vital to realize that with this we have an intrinsic link between a child's physical development and a teacher's moral-ethical development. Steiner points this out in many of his educational lecture courses in sublime simplicity. The last lectures in the following educational courses are particularly relevant: *Foundations of Human Experience* (op. cit.), *The Roots of Education* (op. cit.), *The Essentials of Education* (Anthroposophic Press, Hudson, NY, GA 308), *Education for Adolescence* (op. cit.), *Balance in Teaching* (op. cit., Lecture of September 21, 1920), of which the last is of paramount importance. In these lectures—and in many others—we may find a wealth of indications which enable the teacher to imbue her soul and spirit being with the necessary ideas and inspiration to develop in herself the members of her own organization—etheric, astral, ego, *the spirit self on its path towards manifestation,* in such a way that she may exert a beneficent influence upon her fellow human beings. This teacher may then work also beneficially upon the development of the corresponding lower members of her students.

We shall not dwell any further on these vital indications, as they are part of each teacher's individual and intimate striving. We shall, however, point to another implication of the above quotation.

The Movement Organization and the Impaired Etheric Body

The above quoted lecture makes it abundantly clear that due to the insinuation—ever increasing in our time—of ahrimanic beings into the etheric bodies of human beings, the human soul is dammed up, congested, as it were, without reaching into the very extremities. Hands and feet become clumsy, the soul is stopped up, as it were, at knees and elbows. Outer motion—which indicates the flow of astral currents—is hindered by these beings in our etheric bodies.

Every teacher who has eyes to see must be appalled by the growing clumsiness, by the halting, stumbling gait of many students today, as compared to a decade or two, maybe even a generation, ago! Loving observation makes it obvious that many children, many adults for that matter, do not fully permeate their physical bodies. Further loving observation will bring home to us the crass disparity between soul-filled and soul-void—mechanical—bodily motion.

Let us not forget here that the ability to move, with one's physical, etheric, and astral configurations, is directly related to the ability to arrive at conclusions and make judgments, as described in Chapter 7. One of the consequences of the influence of the two polarizing powers, who aim to paralyze human beings' movement capacities, is an attack upon the intrinsically human ability to learn in a living way, namely by means of the entire body, in contrast to the mere reflection of abstract concepts in the head. Thus the human capacity for experiencing intelligence, which is alive, and may be taken hold of intuitively, is directly attacked by this assault upon the forces of movement. Only coldly, mirrored abstract concepts are not impaired!

Let us enter a little more deeply into this problem. The ahrimanic beings, as they penetrate into our nature, take hold of our intelligence, and begin to think for us, despising us, while also permeating our limbs. Thus human beings become servants of the ahrimanic intentions.

The plight of children is tremendous today. Behaviorist educational philosophy regards a human being as hollow—soul and spirit are non-perceptible to adherents of this philosophy, and so there appears to be a kind of vacuum inside a human being. Steiner mentions in many of his lectures a prior historical attack upon the spiritual essence of each human being, namely the declaration by the Eighth Ecumenical Council in 869 AD, that human beings consist of body and soul, which has some spiritual qualities, but not an independent spirit. The stimulus-response approach puts *garbage into a person*, fills him or her up willy-nilly, and then assumes that these abstract data are stored and able to be recalled. Let us note, at least, the quantitative terminology which is employed by behaviorist methods, remembering that the picture of the learning process as described in these pages takes fully into account that each human being has body, soul and spirit—the eternal essence of his or her inner being.

B. F. Skinner, the most visible proponent of the behaviorist school, states very clearly that all concepts which describe the human being as having an inner self ought to be declared redundant. *Autonomous man* is to be disregarded, for autonomous man cannot be recorded and measured, and thus does not exist.[106] He concludes that inner man must be abolished, for the inner man has been created as the image of the outer. This statement shows clearly with what dangerous illusions we are bombarded today. For modern science sees nothing when directing its attention to the soul. It sees, quite rightly, a vacuum. This is due to the lack of the appropriate instruments for researching into the forces of the soul. Instruments for the soul need to consist of the same nature as the human soul itself—they need to be *soul instruments*. Steiner, in many of his works, shows us how to develop these subtle instruments of our soul forces (for instance in the above-mentioned *The Effects of Esoteric Development*, op. cit.). Because modern materialistic science sees only a vacuum, it declares that there is, in fact, a vacuum. This fallacy rides rampant in various disguises in nineteenth and twentieth century materialistic ideology. It is tantamount to saying that because a person is blind, and thus lacks the tools that show a visual world, this world does not exist. In the case of the blind person we know how other senses replace the missing sense perception. Most modern individuals do not yet know that other tools are necessary, when directing attention to matters of the soul and spirit, and thus they create the fable of a materialistic world. Consequently, the demons, which have been conjured up in modern life through the advance of technology, revenge themselves upon humanity. It must be stated here that what follows should in no way be taken as a condemnation of technology—only as a characterization of the need to understand its origin and forces. If we do not understand technology in all its marvelous aspects thoroughly, we are in danger of becoming its slave.

In behaviorist psychology, a human being is regarded as a more or less well-working computer—another consequence of a technological view of individual and cosmos. One forgets only too easily that the world of technology has been created by humanity itself. It is actually remarkable to realize that elements of the human, but also animal and plant physical bodies and properties, have been used to develop the marvels of the modern world through the dismemberment and externalization of the body into its parts and functions, making each part function independently, and endowing it with energy to create mechanical extensions of man.

Anyone who studies the origin of tools, machines and engines will, upon some pondering, find the precise part and function of the human, animal, and plant physiology and anatomy which is imitated, externalized and serialized, so that labor gets done. Steiner once pointed out that, in actuality, when we translate the amount of labor done by machines into the corresponding number of persons who would be needed to do this work, it seems that many more human beings than are actually incarnated are bound to the earth sphere. In order to be able to develop technology, humanity had to call upon the ahrimanic forces and beings of disintegration—for they offered the possibility of dismembering the ideal and universal image of a human being, and so create the world of machines in its image. Steiner refers to the world of machines as a geological layer which humanity has added to the natural mineral layers of the earth.[107] Now demons hold a grimacing and distorting mirror to a person, and she or he picture him or herself in the form of a computer. Demons revenge themselves for not having been recognized in their spiritual reality by human beings. These beings have power over us, only if we do not recognize them. Steiner points out repeatedly that if one makes the working of Ahriman visible, he loses his power. For example, the design by Steiner of the furnace house at the first Goetheanum, the *Heizhaus*, shows architecturally and sculpturally the very forces which were active in it. It also had to stand by itself. Steiner remarks frequently that humanity will only be on the way to understanding Ahriman, and work consciously with these forces, if train stations, airports and factories are designed to reveal the working of these ahrimanic beings in the world of technology through their very form principles. External form needs to correspond to inner essence, in structures serving technology as well as structures serving spiritual science.

In education we now face children who are already damaged in their etheric organism. There are various stages of this damage, which shows itself at first in nervousness and hyperactivity, and turns progressively into apathy. One can literally see the desperate soul of a child wishing to take full and proper possession of its body, but is unable to do so, for its etheric body is already paralyzed to such a degree that the soul cannot flow freely from limb to limb and stream through, but is dammed up everywhere. This then shows itself in the proliferation of present-day learning and social difficulties.

From our acquaintance with Steiner's Spiritual Science we might be aware that the sphere of movement—our ability to set the body into motion—occurs at the border of soul and body, in the area of the senses. We referred to this at the end of Chapter 8 (see *The Case for Anthroposophy*, op. cit.). The sphere of activity, or volition, as Owen Barfield translates it, adjoins the soul sphere proper. Together with the sphere of the senses, it forms a transition between an individual and the external world. It is for this reason, for instance, that when Rudolf Steiner describes the nature of an infant or toddler, he refers to him or her as a being of both *all will* and also *completely senses*, for both outer will and sensory perception are situated in an intermediary position between humanity and cosmos.

Further, it should be obvious that any over-stimulation of the senses would result in a paralysis of movement. Any substitution of *fake sensory experiences* falsifies perception, introduces obstacles, rocks and lumps, as it were, into this delicate human sheath, where world and soul interpenetrate. Foreign bodies are introduced into it with every fake sensory experience, such as the effects of every radio and television set, every artificial scent and flavor, every artificial fabric (in as far as it attempts to fool one's sense of texture, not if it professes to be openly artificial), which freeze the delicately mobile and naturally impressionable sensitive human sheath. In children, who are not as yet in the position to defend themselves because they are still in the process of developing a qualitative response to their sensory perceptions and their motions, this results in a disastrous interference of their incarnation process. As it takes place in the same region of body and soul, we see also volition and motion directly hampered by this interference of the development of healthy sensory perception. Children's souls—thus poisoned—no longer have a reliable bridge to link themselves to the rest of humanity, nor a reliable measure of comparison to distinguish between real and fake sensory values. As educators—knowing all this—we may strive to find the helpers which will enable us to guide children such that they will be strengthened and become sufficiently alert and strong to continue this battle in later life.

Both the ahrimanic and the luciferic beings interfere in the sensory processes—the former are concerned with the higher senses, the latter with the body, or lower, senses. The former will make of a person an automaton, the latter a mystic. Either brings about an imbalance in the sensory-movement realm. The teacher today has a tremendous task from the viewpoint of spiritual science: to understand, transform, and to battle luciferic and ahrimanic demons, and to create a spiritual space through her or his consciousness and inner work, her or his efforts to understand the spiritual configuration of human beings, so that she or he aids children to develop qualitative values of thinking, of feeling, of volition, of sensation and of motion. Steiner makes this point emphatically in his *Foundations of Human Experience* (op. cit., Lecture of September 4, 1919):

> *To be active with a purpose—these words must sink into our minds if we would be teachers. Now when is a man active without purpose? He is active without purpose, senselessly active, when he acts only in accordance with the demands of his body. He acts with purpose when he acts in accordance with the demands of his environment and not merely in accordance with those of his own body. We must pay heed to this where the child is concerned.*

In the meaningful execution of movement we have a key for the uniting of qualitative values with the soul-spirit being of the child. It must therefore be one of our foremost concerns for children to fill their activities, in every smallest detail of motion, with meaning, thus allowing interest to develop. We shall heal the inroads which today's conditions of civilization have made upon senses and healthy bodily development when we work with such an infusion of meaning into movement activity.

We may also receive help in this battle for human etheric bodies. Rather than describe this help theoretically, I shall put it in story form.

A Fable for Teachers

The air was flush with the promise of summer. Birds chirped and sang, insects hummed, and the sunlight glittered through the green tops of the mighty trees surrounding the house in which a young school had its home. In the distance was the roar of the traffic, for this was in one of the larger cities in America.

A lesson was in progress—recorder playing. Much as the teacher tried, the class seemed more restless than usual. All children who could be relied upon to be restless were so with a vengeance, and the others were given over to their apathetic dreams.

Neither kindness nor cajoling, neither humor nor sternness had any effect. Hardly had one child calmed sufficiently to be ready for work when another took over to *perform*. An imp seemed to jump from child to child—fanning their rebellious actions one by one.

An Imp?

A sad-faced, long and thin, greenish-black being, with pale face and glittering eyes, made the rounds. He attempted to melt his *body*, such as it was, into the bodies of each child in turn. The apathetic ones offered him no resistance—he came and went as if he owned their bodies to house him at his pleasure.

The others, though, they struggled. Restlessly they jerked, agitatedly they pranced about, shouted, giggled, and seemed utterly incapable of heeding the teacher's plea to keep still and quiet. How could they when they were plagued by the green being seeking to take possession of the houses of their souls? How could they when they were being threatened with eviction from their rightful house?

The sight of the green/black being stirred the teacher to anger and pity: "So it is you who undermines my work, who steals the bodies of the children away from their souls, who seeks to insinuate himself into a foreign nest! Who are you? You are lost! You have lost your rightful place in creation. Who has driven you from your own home?"

At first the green/black being made as if to attack the teacher—distorting both face and body in fearful grimace.

The teacher remained calm. "I'll not permit you to contaminate my charges any longer. I have helpers of your own kind who will drive you where you belong. Your place is to keep an engine going, or a pump, or any other motor. But here, where living beings are, you are an intruder."

With earnest determination and iron will the teacher directed a plea to his rightful helpers—the beings of the natural elements. "Come, spirits of flame and fire! Bring your fire of enthusiasm, the glow of interest, the lively and active yearning for transmutation and metamorphosis.

"Come spirits of the air. Sound your melodious rhymes, glance your bright beams of light, and fan the sympathetic ear of my charges, arouse their curiosity; let their thoughts dance in patterns of brightness over the dark spaces of the world; give us of your gentle speech and loving rhyme.

"Come, spirits of water. Stir our feeling for the goodness of this world; let rise and fall the waters of transformation and life; sound out the cycles of birth and death; let them engender awe and love for the world. Come, spirits of earth, you spirits of crystalline certainty—you who give structure and firm form to all that is. Give form and structure to us also, so that understanding may prevail."

Lo and behold—they came. As they came, the green being fled away, but not without an accusing glance at the teacher. "Why," it seemed to ask, "Why do you banish me? Have you not bound me to yourself in the first place?" However, the teacher relegated that question to a later time of contemplation.

The fiery spirits stirred the hearts in enthusiastic response. The earthy beings scattered thoughts like glittering jewels all around. The airy beings scintillated in melodious song and harmonious sense of well-being. The watery beings rolled their soothing waves over the restless emotions and cooled the forbidden fires.

Souls were calmed. Peace reigned. No words were needed to call the class to order. No words were needed to address each unruly child. All worked together. An inner awareness of the battle, which spirits wage with spirits on the stage of the human soul, was needed to restore the balance which human souls need to grow to their fulfillment, just as the plant needs light. The lesson, now restored, was brought to fruition. Meaningful work was done.

The question of the green-black being, however, remained. Why the accusing glance, as he departed? Is humanity guilty of binding him, unredeemed, to the lower rungs of existence?

The Work of the Teacher

Much has been said by Steiner about the inner work of the teacher, about the inner work of each person aspiring to do her or his share in the building of a new world out of the old world of materialism. Though a hundred years into the Michael age, and soon a hundred years into the age of light, we have as yet little outer indication that an upward tilt in the development of humanity has occurred.

The inertia of materialism is strong. Insidious are the ways in which spiritually striving men and women are opposed and foiled in honest attempts to do their share. And, let us not forget it, at least half of the obstacles, hindrances, nay, the attacks, of the opposing powers come from within, from within our very own souls and beings—thus self-knowledge is the sword which hardens the steel of our will and intention. How may we ready ourselves to invoke the beings who are the helpers of humanity in its battle?

To return to the concepts stated by Steiner so succinctly in his *The Case for Anthroposophy*. The battle for an individual's independent existence today is fought in the intermediate zone between inner essence— soul and spirit—and external world. In other words, the battle is fought in the realm of sense and movement activity. As we attempted to demonstrate in the previous chapter, the actual zone in which the temperaments are active in human beings is this very same zone—the transition between body and soul, between each individual and the world.

Sensory and motion activities also take place primarily in this intermediate zone—thus temperament characteristics express themselves, as has already been stated several times above, in filtering our sensory perceptions and coloring our movements and gestures. We work creatively and artistically into this intermediate zone of human existence whenever we speak the language of the temperaments.

In the elementary grades of any school, and particularly in a Waldorf school, we work primarily with the child's senses and movement capacities. The level of this work is threefold:

In the form, gesture, and gestalt aspect of nature and individual;

In the musicality, rhythm, and tempo aspect of nature and individual;

In the color and image quality of nature and individual.

In each of these three areas we may find and use the appropriate and characteristic expressions for each of the four temperaments. Thus, there are twelve possibilities—four modalities on three levels of expression and experience. This twelvefold mode of expression provides us with a wide range of possibilities for developing our approaches to the subject matter in each grade. We need to transform each element of knowledge, each skill, each artistic experience, so that the elemental beings in this intermediate zone between world and individual may help us infuse it with life and meaning.

We have given some examples of how a teacher might work at learning to transform the subject matter so that the four elemental qualities of the temperament modes come to expression. These examples are intended to stimulate teachers to do their own work. After all, each individual teacher might learn to use her or his own self as a tool of education, sharpen the qualitative sensibilities in each of the arts in earnest work, in order that that life-giving powers may work through the teacher's etheric body sculpturally into the physical well-being of students; so that life-giving powers may work through the teacher's astral body painterly into the etheric bodies of students; so that life-giving powers may work musically through the teacher's ego into the astral bodies of the students; so that life-giving powers may work poetically through the teacher's (potential) spirit self into the egos of the students. If we strive towards this, we are at work to redeem the arts in our time, and, in so doing, begin to create an outer indication that an upward tilt in the development of humanity can occur.

The Redemption of the Arts

The arts are intrinsically involved in this intermediate zone of senses and volition, of motion. The fourfold quality of the elements finds its expression in each art. Through each art a different member of the human constitution may be permeated with spiritual life, and thus be strengthened to withstand the divisive and death-dealing forces which are abroad in our technological culture.

Through art—artistic experience enlivened by the four temperament-element modes—we redeem also the image of the universal human. What else could Steiner have meant when describing the New Isis legend? Horus—the image of man—is torn apart by Typhon and restored to Isis by the elemental beings of nature:

> *Thus the new Isis had carried her offspring into the world and the world had dismembered it in fourteen pieces. When the spirit-visitor, the new Typhon, had come to know of this, he gathered together the fourteen pieces, and with all the knowledge of natural, scientific profundity he again made a being, a single whole, out of the fourteen pieces. But in this being there were only mechanical laws, the law of the machine. . . . Thus a being had arisen with the appearance of life but with the laws of the machine. And since this being had arisen out of fourteen pieces, it could reproduce itself again, fourteenfold. And Typhon could give a reflection of his own being to each piece, so that each of the fourteen offspring of the new Isis had a countenance that resembled the new Typhon.*

> *And Isis had to follow all this strange affair, half divining it; half divining she could see the whole miraculous change that had come to her offspring. She knew that she had herself dragged it about, that she had herself brought all this to pass. But there came a day when in its true, its genuine form she could accept it again from a group of spirits who were elemental spirits of nature, could receive it from nature elementals.*

> *As she received her true offspring which only through an illusion had been stamped into the offspring of Typhon, there dawned upon her a remarkable clairvoyant vision: She suddenly noticed that she still had the cow-horns of ancient Egypt, in spite of having become a new Isis.*

Through the strength of her clairvoyance, there one day arose in her the deep meaning, as far as the age could reach, of that which is described in St. John's Gospel as the Logos. There arose in her the Johannine significance of the Mystery of Golgotha. Through this strength the power of the cow-horns grasped the paper crown and changed it into an actual golden crown of genuine substance.[108]

When engaged in teaching as intended by Steiner, we are directly concerned with the redemption of Horus—the universal image of the human being—from dismemberment by Typhon. Our striving to create dynamic equilibrium between the two adversaries (Lucifer and Ahriman) enables the elemental beings of nature to come to our aid. Then we may contribute to the eventual rising of a new spiritual culture out of the ashes of materialism.

Endnotes:

[1] Rudolf Steiner, *The Human Soul in Relation to World Evolution,* Anthroposophic Press, Spring Valley, NY, 1984, GA 112, Lecture of May 26, 1922.

[2] Caroline von Heydebrand, *Childhood,* A Study of the Growing Soul, Anthroposophical Publishing Co., London, 1942.

[3] Walter Scott, Editor, *Corpus Hermeticum,* the ancient Greek and Latin writings which contain religious and philosophic teachings ascribed to Hermes Trismegistus, edited with English translation and notes, Oxford, Clarendon Press, 1924.

[4] See Rudolf Steiner, *An Outline of Esoteric Science,* Anthroposophic Press, Hudson, NY, 1997, GA 13, for descriptions of these past stages of earth evolution in Chapter 4.

[5] Rudolf Steiner, *Mysterienwahrheiten und Weihnachtsimpulse,* Rudolf Steiner Verlag, Dornach, Switzerland, 1980, GA 180, Lecture of December 30, 1917 (translated by author)

[6] Rudolf Steiner, *Mysterienwahrheiten und Weihnachtsimpulse,* op.cit.

[7] Ibid.

[8] Rudolf Steiner, *The Recovery of the Living Source of Speech,* The Golden Blade, ed. Adam Bittleston, Rudolf Steiner Press, London, 1973, GA224, Lecture of April 13, 1923.

[9] Rudolf Steiner, *Cosmic Memory. Atlantis and Lemuria,* Rudolf Steiner Publications, Blauvelt, NY, 1971, GA 11.

[10] Rudolf Steiner, *The Recovery of the Living Source of Speech,* op.cit.

[11] Rudolf Steiner, *World History in the Light of Anthroposophy,* Rudolf Steiner Press, London, 1977, GA233, Lecture of December 24, 1923.

[12] Steiner pinpoints the moment in history when this change occurred as the span of time between Plato and Aristotle. See also *The Recovery of the Living Source of Speech,* op.cit.

[13] Ibid.

[14] Rudolf Steiner, *Speech and Drama,* Anthroposophic Press, Spring Valley, NY, 1986, GA 282, Lecture of September 21, 1924.

[15] Rudolf Steiner, *Foundations of Human Experience,* Anthroposophic Press, Hudson, NY, 1996, GA 293, Lecture of August 27, 1919.

[16] Rudolf Steiner, *The Boundaries of Natural Science,* Anthroposophic Press, Spring Valley, NY, 1983, GA 322, Lecture of October 3, 1920.

[17] Rudolf Steiner, *Education for Adolescence,* Anthroposophic Press, Hudson, NY, 1996, GA 302, Lecture of June 14, 1921.

[18] Rudolf Steiner, *True and False Paths in Spiritual Investigation,* Rudolf Steiner Press, London, 1969, GA 243, Lecture of August 20, 1924.

[19] Ibid.

[20] Rudolf Steiner, *Art as Seen in the Light of Mystery Wisdom,* Rudolf Steiner Press, London, 1996, GA 275, Lecture of December 29, 1914.

[21] Rudolf Steiner, *The Riddle of Humanity,* Rudolf Steiner Press, London, 1990, GA 170, Lecture of August 15, 1916.

[22] Ibid.

[23] Rudolf Steiner, *The Riddle of Humanity,* op. cit.

[24] Rudolf Steiner, *The Riddle of Humanity,* op. cit., lecture of September 2, 1916.

[25] Rudolf Steiner, *Man as a Being of Sense and Perception,* Anthroposophical Publishing Company, London, 1958, GA 206, Lecture of July 22, 1921.

[26] Ibid. Lecture of July 23, 1921.

[27] Rudolf Steiner, *Toward Imagination, Culture and the Individual,* Anthroposophic Press, Hudson, HY, 1990, GA 169, Lecture of June 13, 1916.

[28] Rudolf Steiner, *Man as a Being of Sense and Perception,* op.cit. Lecture of July 23, 1921.

[29] Rudolf Steiner, *Esoteric Christianity and the Mission of Christian Rosenkreutz,* Anthroposophic Press, Hudson, NY, 2001, GA 130, Lecture of December 18, 1912.

[30] Rudolf Steiner, *True and False Paths...,* op. cit. Lecture of August 22, 1924.

[31] Rudolf Steiner, *Art as Seen in the Light of Mystery Wisdom,* op.cit. Lecture of December 29, 1914.

[32] Rudolf Steiner, *Fall and Redemption,* Mercury Press, Spring Valley, NY, 1995, GA 220, Lecture of January 19, 1923, entitled *Truth, Beauty and Goodness.*

[33] Rudolf Steiner, *Cosmic Prehistoric Ages of Mankind,* Manuscript from Rudolf Steiner Library, from *Das Geschichtsleben der Menschheit,* Rudolf Steiner Verlag, Dornach, Switzerland, GA 184, Lecture of September 20, 1918.

[34] Rudolf Steiner, *The Spiritual Ground of Education,* Anthroposophical Publishing Co., London, 1947, GA 305, Lecture of August 21, 1922.

[35] Rudolf Steiner, *Discussion with Teachers,* Rudolf Steiner Press, London, 1983, GA 295, Lecture of August 25, 1919.

[36] Rudolf Steiner, *The Relationship of Various Natural Sciences to Astronomy,* typescript only, available from Rudolf Steiner Library, Ghent, NY, GA 323, Lecture of January 15, 1921.

[37] Rudolf Steiner, *Art as Seen in the Light of Mystery Wisdom,* op. cit., Lecture of September 12, 1920.

[38] Rudolf Steiner, *Art as Seen in the Light of Mystery Wisdom,* op. cit., Lecture of December 29, 1914.

[39] Rudolf Steiner, *The Bhagavad Gita and the Epistles of St. Paul,* Anthroposophic Press, Spring Valley, NY, 1971, GA 142, Lecture of December 29, 1912.

[40] Rudolf Steiner, *Colour,* Rudolf Steiner Press, London, 1992, GA 291, Lecture of May 8, 1921.

[41] Ibid., Lecture of May 7, 1921.

[42] Rudolf Steiner, *The Cycle of the Year,* Anthroposophic Press, Spring Valley, NY, 1984, GA 223, Lecture of April 2, 1923.

[43] Contained in Rudolf Steiner, *Colour,* Rudolf Steiner Press, edition of 1971, Appendix: Extracts from Rudolf Steiner's Notebooks.

[44] Liliane Collot D'Herbois, *Colour,* Stichting Magenta, Driebergen, The Netherlands, 1979.

[45] E. A. Karl Stockmeyer, *Rudolf Steiner's Curriculum for Waldorf Schools,* Steiner Schools Fellowship, 1969, Distributed by Rudolf Steiner Press, London, p. 199.

[46] Rudolf Steiner, *Colour,* op. cit., Lecture of May 7, 1921.

[47] Rudolf Steiner, *Art as Seen in the Light of Mystery Wisdom,* op. cit., Lecture of September 12, 1920.

[48] Rudolf Steiner, *Art as Seen in the Light of Mystery Wisdom,* op. cit., Lecture of September 12, 1920.

[49] Rudolf Steiner, *Art as Seen in the Light of Mystery Wisdom,* op. cit., Lecture of December 29, 1914.

[50] Rudolf Steiner, *True and False Paths,* op. cit. Lecture of August 22, 1924

[51] Ibid.

[52] Rudolf Steiner, *Balance in Teaching,* Mercury Press, Spring Valley, NY, 1982, GA 302a, Lecture of September 21, 1920.

[53] Rudolf Steiner, *The Child's Changing Consciousness and Waldorf Education,* Anthroposophic Press, Hudson, NY, 1988, GA 306, Lecture of April 22, 1923.

[54] Rudolf Steiner, *Art as Seen in the Light of Mystery Wisdom,* op. cit. Lecture of March 7, 1923.

[55] Rudolf Steiner, *Eurythmy as Visible Music,* Rudolf Steiner Press, London, 1977, GA 278, Lecture of February 21, 1924.

[56] Rudolf Steiner, *True and False Paths...* op. cit. Lecture of August 22, 1924.

[57] Rudolf Steiner, *The Influences of Lucifer and Ahriman,* Man's Responsibility for the Earth, Steiner Book Centre, Inc., North Vancouver, Canada, 1976, GA 191, Lecture of November 15, 1919.

[58] Rudolf Steiner, *The Younger Generation,* Anthroposophic Press, Spring Valley, NY, 1976, GA 217, Lecture of October 12, 1922.

[59] Rudolf Steiner, *World History in the Light of Anthroposophy,* op. cit. Lecture of December 27, 1923.

[60] Rudolf Steiner, *A Psychology of Body, Soul and Spirit,* Anthroposophic Press, Hudson, NY, 1999, GA 115, Lecture of October 26, 1909.

[61] Rudolf Steiner, *The Riddle of Humanity,* op. cit. Lecture of September 2, 1916.

[62] Rudolf Steiner, *Foundations of Human Experience,* Anthroposophic Press, Hudson, NY, 1996, GA 293, Lecture of August 27, 1919.

[63] Rudolf Steiner, *Therapeutic Insights. Earthly and Cosmic Laws,* Mercury Press, Spring Valley, NY, 1984, GA 205, Lecture of July 3, 1921.

[64] Rudolf Steiner, *Art as Seen in the Light of Mystery Wisdom,* op. cit., Lecture of December 29, 1914.

[65] Rudolf Steiner, *Adolescence. Ripe for What?,* Steiner Schools Fellowship, Forest Row, England, UK, 1996, GA 302, Lecture of June 22, 1922.

[66] Rudolf Steiner, *Education for Adolescence,* Anthroposophic Press, Hudson, NY, 1996, GA 302, Lecture of June 14, 1921.

[67] Rudolf Steiner, *Speech and Drama,* op. cit. Lecture of September 12, 1924.

[68] Rudolf Steiner, *The Arts and Their Mission,* Anthroposophic Press, Spring Valley, NY, 1967, GA 276, Lecture of May 20, 1923.

[69] Rudolf Steiner, Marie Steiner-von Sievers, *Creative Speech. The Nature of Speech Formation,* Rudolf Steiner Press, London, 1978, GA 280, p. 209.

[70] Rudolf Steiner, *Speech and Drama,* op. cit., Lecture of September 21, 1924.

[71] Rudolf Steiner, *Creative Speech,* op.cit., p. 159.

[72] Rudolf Steiner, *Art as Seen in the Light of Mystery Wisdom,* Rudolf Steiner Press, London, GA 275, Lecture of January 2, 1915: *Working with Sculptural Architecture.*

[73] Rudolf Steiner, *Speech and Drama,* op. cit., Lecture of September 7, 1924.

[74] Rudolf Steiner, *The Tension Between East and West,* Anthroposophic Press, Spring Valley, NY, 1983, GA 83, Chapter 5.

[75] Rudolf Steiner, *The World of the Senses and the World of the Spirit,* Steiner Book Centre, Inc. North Vancouver, Canada, 1979, GA 134, Lecture of December 30, 1911.

[76] Rudolf Steiner, *The Roots of Education,* Anthroposophic Press, Hudson, NY, 1997, GA 309, Lecture of April 14, 1924.

[77] Rudolf Steiner, *Agriculture,* Biodynamic Agricultural Association, Rudolf Steiner House, London, 1974, GA 327, Lecture of June 11, 1924.

[78] Rudolf Steiner, *Education for Special Needs,* The Curative Education Course, Rudolf Steiner Press, London, 1998, GA 317, Lecture of July 7, 1924.

[79] Rudolf Steiner, *The Bridge between Universal Spirituality and the Physical Constitution of Man,* The Anthroposophic Press, Spring Valley, NY, 1979, Lecture of December 18, 1920.

[80] Rudolf Steiner, *Foundations of Human Experience,* op. cit., Lecture of August 22, 1919.

[81] Rudolf Steiner, *Cosmosophy. Cosmic Influences on the Human Being,* Volume 1, Anthroposophic Press, Hudson, NY, 1985, GA 207, Lecture of October 9, 1921.

[82] Rudolf Steiner, *Education for Special Needs,* op. cit.

[83] Rudolf Steiner, *The Human Soul in Relation to World Evolution,* op. cit.

[84] Rudolf Steiner, *The Case for Anthroposophy,* Selections from *Von Seelenraetseln,* translated by Owen Barfield, Rudolf Steiner Press, London, 1970, Chapter 7.

[85] Rudolf Steiner, *Cosmosophy,* Volume 2, Completion Press, Gympie, Australia, 1997, GA 208, Lecture of October 30, 1921.

[86] Rudolf Steiner, *The Case for Anthroposophy,* op. cit.

[87] Ibid.

[88] Rudolf Steiner, *Anthroposophy in Everyday Life,* "The Four Temperaments," Anthroposophic Press, Hudson, NY, 1995, GA 57.

[89] Rudolf Steiner, *The World of the Senses and the World of the Spirit,* op. cit, Lecture of December 29, 1911.

[90] Ibid., Lecture of December 30, 1911.

[91] Ibid.

[92] Rudolf Steiner, *Agriculture,* op.cit., Lecture of June 10, 1924.

[93] Ibid.

[94] Rudolf Steiner, *Spiritual Science and Medicine,* Rudolf Steiner Press, London, 1975, GA 312, Lecture of March 26, 1920.

[95] Rudolf Steiner, *The Bridge between Universal Spirituality and the Physical Constitution of Man,* op. cit., Lecture of December 17, 1920.

[96] Rudolf Steiner, *Die Verantwortung des Menschen fur die Weltentwicklung,* op. cit., Lecture of March 11, 1921.

[97] Rudolf Steiner, *Speech and Drama,* op. cit., Lecture of September 21, 1924.

[98] Rudolf Steiner, *Art in the Light of Mystery Wisdom,* op. cit., Lecture of March 7, 1923.

[99] Rudolf Steiner, *Education for Special Needs,* op. cit.., Lecture of June 26, 1924.

[100] Rudolf Steiner, *Der Mensch als Gedankenwesen. Kosmische Gestaltungskrafte,* GA 205, Lecture of July 15, 1921.

[101] Rudolf Steiner, *The Effects of Esoteric Development,* Anthroposophic Press, Hudson, NY, GA 145, Lecture of March 25, 1913.

[102] Ibid., Lecture of March 22, 1913.

[103] Rudolf Steiner, *Balance in World and Man,* op. cit., Lecture of November 22, 1914.

[104] Ibid. Lecture of November 20, 1914.

[105] Rudolf Steiner, *Education for Special Needs,* op. cit., Lecture of June 26, 1924.

[106] B. F. Skinner, *Beyond Freedom and Dignity,* A Bantam/Vintage Book, Vintage Books, NY, 1972, particularly chapters 1 and 9.

[107] Rudolf Steiner, *Die Verantwortung des Menschen fur die Weltentwicklung,* op. cit., Lecture of January 30, 1921.

[108] Rudolf Steiner, *Ancient Myths. Their Meaning and Connection to Evolution,* Steiner Book Centre, North Vancouver, Canada, 1978, GA 180, Lecture of January 6, 1918.

Bibliography

Chomski, Noam. *Language and Mind,* Harcourt Brace Jovanovich, Inc., New York: 1972.

Collot D'Herbois, Liliane. *Colour, Part I,* Stichting Driebergen, Magenta, The Netherlands: 1979.

Heidebrand, Caroline von. *Childhood A Study of the Growing Soul,* Anthroposophical Publishing Co. London: 1942.

Scott, Walter, ed. *Corpus Hermeticum,* the ancient Greek and Latin writings which contain religious and philosophic teachings ascribed to Hermes Trismegistus, edited with English translation and notes, Oxford: Clarendon Press, 1924.

Steiner, Rudolf. *Adolescence: Ripe for What?* Steiner Schools Fellowship, Forest Row, England: 1996, Lecture of June 22, 1922.

_____ . *Agriculture,* Biodynamic Agricultural Association, Rudolf Steiner House, London: 1974, GA 327, Lecture of June 11, 1924.

_____ . *Anthroposophy in Everyday Life,* The Four Temperaments, Anthroposophic Press, GA 57, Hudson, New York: 1995.

_____ . *Art as Seen in the Light of Mystery Wisdom,* Rudolf Steiner Press, London: 1996, GA 275, Lecture of December 29, 1914 , *The Bearing of Spiritual Science on Art,* Lecture of January 2, 1915, *Working with Sculptural Architecture I,* Lecture of September 12, 1920, *The Supersensible Origin of the Artistic.*

_____ . *The Arts and Their Mission,* Anthroposophic Press, Hudson, New York: 1967, GA 276, Lecture of May 20, 1923.

_____ . *Balance in Teaching,* Mercury Press, Spring Valley, New York: 1982, GA 302a, Lectures of September 12, 1920 and September 21, 1920.

_____ . *The Bhagavad Gita and the Epistles of St. Paul,* Anthroposophic Press, Hudson, New York: 1971, GA 142, Lecture of December 29, 1912.

_____ . *The Boundaries of Natural Science,* Anthroposophic Press , Hudson, New York: 1983, GA 322, Lecture of October 3, 1920.

_____ . *The Bridge between Universal Spirituality and the Physical Constitution of Man,* Anthroposophic Press, Spring Valley, New York: 1979, Lecture of December 18, 1920.

_____ . *The Case for Anthroposophy*, selections from Von Seelenraetseln, translated by Owen Barfield, Chapter 7, Rudolf Steiner Press, London, 1970.

_____ . *Das Geschichtsleben der Menschheit*, Rudolf Steiner Verlag, English in Manuscript, "Cosmic Prehistoric Ages of Mankind," Dornach, Switzerland: GA 184, Lecture of September 20, 1918.

_____ . *The Child's Changing Consciousness and Waldorf Education*, Anthroposophic Press, Hudson, New York: 1988, GA 306, Lecture of April 22, 1923.

_____ . *Colour*, Rudolf Steiner Press, London: 1992, GA 291, Lecture of May 8, 1921.

_____ . *Colour*, GA 291, Appendix: Extracts from *Rudolf Steiner's Notebooks*, Rudolf Steiner Press, London: 1971.

_____ . *Cosmic Memory*. Atlantis and Lemuria, Rudolf Steiner Publications, GA 11, Blauvelt, New York: 1971.

_____ . *Cosmosophy, Cosmic Influences on the Human Being, Vol 1*, Anthroposophic Press, Hudson, New York: 1985, GA 207, Lecture of October 9, 1921.

_____ . *Cosmosophy, Cosmic Influences on the Human Being, Vol 2*, Completion Press, Gympie, Australia: 1997, GA 207, Lecture of October 30, 1921.

_____ . *The Cycle of the Year*, Anthroposophic Press, Hudson, New York: 1984, GA 223, Lecture of April 2, 1923.

_____ . *Discussions with Teachers*, Anthroposophic Press, Hudson, New York: 1997, GA 295, Lecture of August 21, 1919.

_____ . *Education for Adolescence*, Anthroposophic Press, GA 302, Hudson, New York: 1996.

_____ . *Education for Special Needs: The Curative Education Course*, Rudolf Steiner Press, London: 1998, GA 317, Lecture of July 7, 1924.

_____ . *The Effects of Esoteric Development*, Anthroposophic Press, Hudson, New York: 1997, Lectures of March 22 and 25, 1913.

_____ . *Esoteric Christianity and the Mission of Christian Rosenkreutz*, Anthroposophic Press, Hudson, New York: 2000, GA 130, Lecture of December 18, 1912.

_____ . *Eurythmy as Visible Music*, Rudolf Steiner Press, London: 1977, GA 278, Lecture of February 21, 1924.

_____ . *Fall and Redemption*, Mercury Press, GA 220, Lecture of January 19, 1923, entitled "Truth, Beauty and Goodness," Spring Valley, New York: 1995.

_____ . *Foundations of Human Experience*, Anthroposophic Press, Hudson, New York: 1996, GA 293, Lecture of August 27, 1919.

_____ . *The Human Soul in Relation to World Evolution*, Anthroposophic Press, GA 112, Hudson, New York: 1984.

_____ . *The Influences of Lucifer and Ahriman, Man's Responsibility for the Earth*, Steiner Book Centre, North Vancouver, Canada: 1976, Lecture of November 15, 1919.

_____ . *Intuitive Thinking as a Spiritual Path*, formerly titled *Philosophy of Spiritual Activity*, GA 4, Hudson, New York: Anthroposophic Press.

_____ . *Man as a Being of Sense and Perception*, Anthroposophical Publishing Company, London: 1958, GA 206, Lecture of July 22, 1921.

_____ . *Man as Symphony of the Creative Word*, Rudolf Steiner Press, London: 1970, GA 230, Lecture of November 11, 1923.

_____ . *Der Mensch als Gedankenwesen. Kosmische Gestaltungskrafte*, Lecture of July 15, 1921.

_____ . *The Mission of the Archangel Michael: His Mission and Ours*, Anthroposophic Press, Hudson, New York: 1994.

_____ . *Mysterienwahrheiten und Weihnachtsimpulse*, Rudolf Steiner Verlag, GA 180, Lecture of December 30, 1917, Dornach, Switzerland: 1980.

_____ . *Mystery Knowledge and Mystery Centres*, Rudolf Steiner Press, London.

_____ . *An Outline of Esoteric Science*, Anthroposophic Press, GA 13, Hudson, New York: 1997.

_____ . *A Psychology of Body, Soul and Spirit*, Anthroposophic Press, Hudson, New York: 1999, GA 115, Lecture of October 26, 1909.

_____ . *The Relationship of Various Natural Sciences to Astronomy*, typescript only, available from Rudolf Steiner Library, Ghent, New York: GA 323, Lecture of January 15, 1921.

_____ . *The Riddle of Humanity*, Rudolf Steiner Press, London: 1990, GA 170, Lecture of August 15, 1916.

_____ . *The Roots of Education*, Anthroposophic Press, Hudson, New York: 1997, GA 309, Lecture of April 14, 1924.

_____ . *Speech and Drama*, Anthroposophic Press, Hudson, New York: 1986, GA 282, Lecture of September 21, 1924.

_____ . *The Spiritual Ground of Education*, Anthroposophical Publishing Co. London: 1947, GA 305, Lecture of August 21, 1922.

_____ . *Spiritual Science and Medicine*, Rudolf Steiner Press, London: 1975, Lecture of March 26, 1920.

_____ . *The Tension Between East and West*, Anthroposophic Press, Chapter 5, Hudson, New York: 1983.

_____ . *Theosophy*, Anthroposophic Press, Hudson, New York: 1994.

_____ . *Therapeutic Insights: Earthly and Cosmic Laws*, Mercury Press, Spring Valley, New York: 1984, GA 205, Lecture of July 3, 1921.

_____ . *Toward Imagination, Culture and the Individual*, Anthroposophic Press, Hudson, New York: 1990, GA 169, Lecture of June 13, 1916.

_____ . *True and False Paths in Spiritual Investigation*, Rudolf Steiner Press, GA 243, London: 1969.

_____ . *World History in the Light of Anthroposophy*, Rudolf Steiner Press, London: 1977, GA 233, Lecture of December 24, 1923.

_____ . *The World of the Senses and the World of the Spirit*, Steiner Book Centre Inc., North Vancouver, Canada: 1979, GA 134, Lecture of December 30, 1911.

_____ . *The Younger Generation*, Anthroposophic Press, Hudson, New York: 1976, GA 217, Lecture of October 12, 1922.

_____ . "The Recovery of the Living Source of Speech," *The Golden Blade*, ed. Adam Bittleston, Rudolf Steiner Press, London: 1973, GA224, Lecture of April 13, 1923.

_____ , and Marie Steiner-von Sievers. *Creative Speech. The Nature of Speech Formation*, Rudolf Steiner Press, GA 280, p. 209, London: 1978.

Stockmeyer, E. A. Karl. *Rudolf Steiner's Curriculum for Waldorf Schools*, Steiner Schools Fellowship, Forest Row, England, 1969, p. 199.